Isaiah

Part One

Isaiah

Part One

Isaiah 1–39

Leslie J. Hoppe

with Little Rock Scripture Study staff

Little Rock
Scripture Study

LITURGICAL PRESS
Collegeville, Minnesota

www.littlerockscripture.org

This symbol indicates material that was created by Little Rock Scripture Study to supplement the biblical text and commentary. Some of these inserts first appeared in the *Little Rock Catholic Study Bible*; others were created specifically for this book by Michael DiMassa.

1   2   3   4   5   6   7   8   9

Library of Congress Cataloging-in-Publication Data

Names: Hoppe, Leslie J., author. | Little Rock Scripture Study Staff, author.
Title: Isaiah / Leslie J. Hoppe with Little Rock Scripture Study staff.
Description: Collegeville, MN : Liturgical Press, [2023-] | Completed in 2 volumes. | Contents: v. 1. Isaiah 1-39 — v. 2. Isaiah 40-66. | Summary: "A Bible study on the book of Isaiah exploring the history, theology, and poetry of this prophetic work. Includes commentary, study and reflection questions, prayers, and access to online lectures"— Provided by publisher.
Identifiers: LCCN 2022028476 (print) | LCCN 2022028477 (ebook) | ISBN 9780814667118 (v. 1 ; trade paperback) | ISBN 9780814667149 (v. 2 ; trade paperback) | ISBN 9780814667132 (v. 1 ; epub) | ISBN 9780814667132 (v. 1 ; pdf) | ISBN 9780814667163 (v. 2 ; epub) | ISBN 9780814667163 (v. 2 ; pdf)
Subjects: LCSH: Bible. Isaiah—Textbooks.
Classification: LCC BS1515.55 .H67 2023 (print) | LCC BS1515.55 (ebook) |
    DDC 224/.106—dc23/eng/20220801
LC record available at https://lccn.loc.gov/2022028476
LC ebook record available at https://lccn.loc.gov/2022028477

TABLE OF CONTENTS

Wrap-Up Lectures and Discussion Tips for Facilitators are available for each lesson at no charge. Find them online at LittleRockScripture.org/Lectures/IsaiahPartOne.

Welcome

The Bible is at the heart of what it means to be a Christian. It is the Spirit-inspired word of God for us. It reveals to us the God who created, redeemed, and guides us still. It speaks to us personally and as a church. It forms the basis of our public liturgical life and our private prayer lives. It urges us to live worthily and justly, to love tenderly and wholeheartedly, and to be a part of building God's kingdom here on earth.

Though it was written a long time ago, in the context of a very different culture, the Bible is no relic of the past. Catholic biblical scholarship is among the best in the world, and in our time and place, we have unprecedented access to it. By making use of solid scholarship, we can discover much about the ancient culture and religious practices that shaped those who wrote the various books of the Bible. With these insights, and by praying with the words of Scripture, we allow the words and images to shape us as disciples. By sharing our journey of faithful listening to God's word with others, we have the opportunity to be stretched in our understanding and to form communities of love and learning. Ultimately, studying and praying with God's word deepens our relationship with Christ.

Isaiah, Part One
Isaiah 1–39

The resource you hold in your hands is divided into six lessons. Each lesson involves personal prayer and study using this book and the experience of group prayer, discussion, and wrap-up lecture.

If you are using this resource in the context of a small group, we suggest that you meet six times, discussing one lesson per meeting. Allow about 90 minutes for the small group gathering. Small groups function best with eight to twelve people to ensure good group dynamics and to allow all to participate as they wish.

Some groups choose to have an initial gathering before their regular sessions begin. This allows an opportunity to meet one another, pass out books, and, if desired, view the optional intro lecture for this study available on the "Resources" page of the Little Rock Scripture Study website (www.littlerockscripture.org). Please note that there is only one intro lecture for two-part studies.

Every Bible study group is a little bit different. Some of our groups like to break each lesson up into two weeks of study so they are reading less each week and have more time to discuss the questions together at their weekly gatherings.

If your group wishes to do this, simply agree how much of each lesson will be read each week, and only answer the questions that correspond to the material you read. Wrap-up lectures can then be viewed at the end of every other meeting rather than at the end of every meeting. Of course, this will mean that your study will last longer, and your group will meet more times.

WHAT MATERIALS WILL YOU USE?

The materials in this book include:

- The text of Isaiah, chapters 1–39, using the New American Bible, Revised Edition as the translation.

- Commentary by Leslie J. Hoppe (which has also been published separately as part of the New Collegeville Bible Commentary series).

- Occasional inserts ❦ highlighting elements of the chapters of Isaiah being studied. Some of these appear also in the *Little Rock Catholic Study Bible* while others are supplied by staff writers.

- Questions for study, reflection, and discussion at the end of each lesson.

- Opening and closing prayers for each lesson, as well as other prayer forms available in the closing pages of the book.

In addition, there are wrap-up lectures available for each lesson. Your group may choose to purchase a DVD containing these lectures or make use of the video lectures available online at no charge. The link to these free lectures is: LittleRockScripture.org/Lectures/IsaiahPartOne. Of course, if your group has access to qualified speakers, you may choose to have live presentations.

Each person will need a current translation of the Bible. We recommend the *Little Rock Catholic Study Bible*, which makes use of the New American Bible, Revised Edition. Other translations, such as the New Jerusalem Bible or the New Revised Standard Version: Catholic Edition, would also work well.

HOW WILL YOU USE THESE MATERIALS?

Prepare in advance

Using Lesson One as an example:

- Begin with a simple prayer like the one found on page 13.

- Read the assigned material for Lesson One (pages 14–25) so that you are prepared for the weekly small group session.
- Answer the questions, Exploring Lesson One, found at the end of the assigned reading, pages 26–28.
- Use the Closing Prayer on page 28 when you complete your study. This prayer may be used again when you meet with the group.

Meet with your small group

- After introductions and greetings, allow time for prayer (about 5 minutes) as you begin the group session. You may use the prayer on page 13 (also used by individuals in their preparation) or use a prayer of your choosing.
- Spend about 45–50 minutes discussing the responses to the questions that were prepared in advance. You may also develop your discussion further by responding to questions and interests that arise during the discussion and faith-sharing itself.
- Close the discussion and faith-sharing with prayer, about 5–10 minutes. You may use the Closing Prayer at the end of each lesson or one of your choosing at the end of the book. It is important to allow people to pray for personal and community needs and to give thanks for how God is moving in your lives.
- Listen to or view the wrap-up lecture associated with each lesson (15–20 minutes). You may watch the lecture online, use a DVD, or provide a live lecture by a qualified local speaker. View the lecture together at the end of the session or, if your group runs out of time, you may invite group members to watch the lecture on their own time after the discussion.

A note to individuals

- If you are using this resource for individual study, simply move at your own pace. Take as much time as you need to read, study, and pray with the material.
- If you would like to share this experience with others, consider inviting a friend or family member to join you for your next study. Even a small group of two or three provides an opportunity for fruitful dialog and faith-sharing!

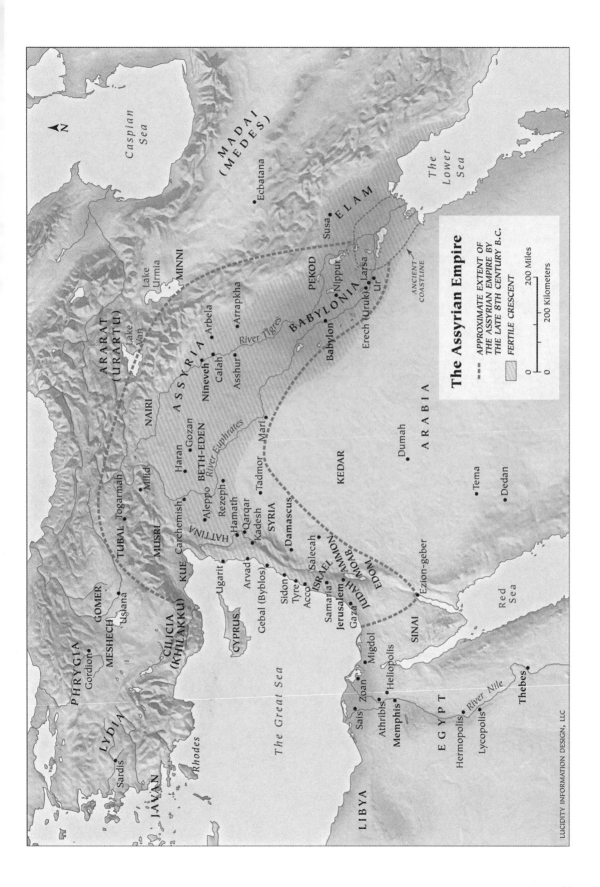

The Assyrian Empire

- - - APPROXIMATE EXTENT OF
THE ASSYRIAN EMPIRE BY
THE LATE 8TH CENTURY B.C.

FERTILE CRESCENT

0 — 200 Miles
0 — 200 Kilometers

LUCIDITY INFORMATION DESIGN, LLC

11

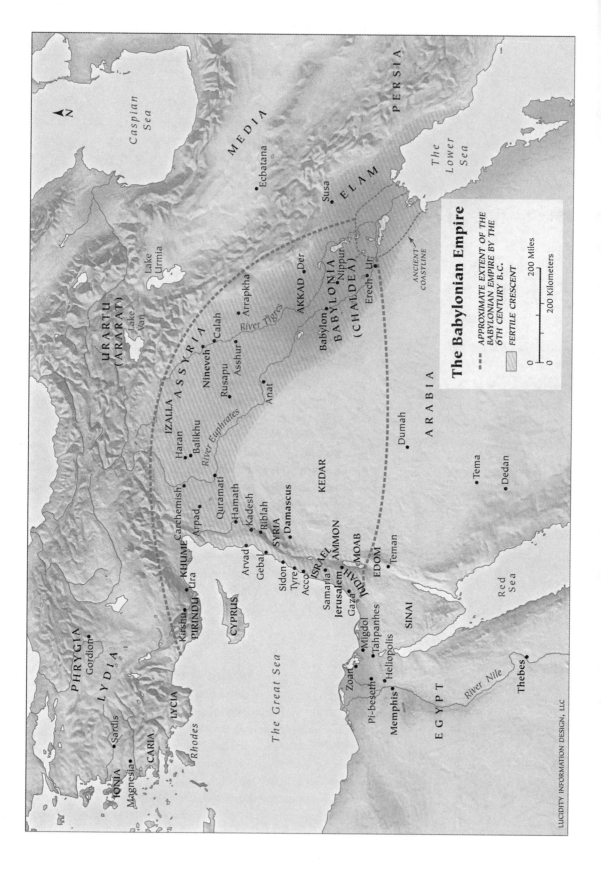

The Babylonian Empire

- - - APPROXIMATE EXTENT OF THE BABYLONIAN EMPIRE BY THE 6TH CENTURY B.C.

FERTILE CRESCENT

0   200 Miles

0   200 Kilometers

N

Caspian Sea

MEDIA

PERSIA

Ecbatana

Susa

ELAM

The Lower Sea

ANCIENT COASTLINE

AKKAD Der

Nippur

BABYLONIA (CHALDEA)

Babylon Erech Ur

Lake Urmia

Lake Van

URARTU (ARARAT)

IZALLA ASSYRIA

Nineveh Calah

Rusapu Asshur

Arrapkha

River Tigres

Anat

River Euphrates

Haran Balikhu

Carchemish

Quramati

Arpad

Hamath

Kadesh

Riblah

SYRIA Damascus

KEDAR

ARABIA

Dumah

Tema

Dedan

Arvad

Gebal

Sidon

Tyre

Acco

Samaria

Jerusalem

Gaza

AMMON

ISRAEL

JUDAH MOAB

EDOM

Teman

Red Sea

SINAI

Migdol

Tahpanhes

Heliopolis

Zoan

Pi-beseth

Memphis

River Nile

Thebes

EGYPT

KHUME

Ura

Kirshu

PIRINDU

CYPRUS

PHRYGIA

Gordion

LYDIA

Sardis

CARIA

LYCIA

IONIA

Magnesia

Rhodes

The Great Sea

Isaiah

Part One

LESSON ONE

Introduction and Isaiah 1–4

Begin your personal study and group discussion with a simple and sincere prayer such as:

Prayer

Heavenly Father, as we read the words of your prophet Isaiah, help us respond to his call to repentance and a new way of life. May our study inspire us to imitate you, the pillar of justice and the fountain of all mercy.

Read the Introduction on pages 14–16 and the Bible text of Isaiah 1–4 found in the outside columns of pages 17–25, highlighting what stands out to you.

Read the accompanying commentary to add to your understanding.

Respond to the questions on pages 26–28, Exploring Lesson One.

The Closing Prayer on page 28 is for your personal use and may be used at the end of group discussion.

INTRODUCTION

By any measure, the book of Isaiah is among the world's greatest works of religious literature. It probes the mystery of a people's life with God. It is unrelenting in its insistence that the foundation of that life is God's commitment to Jerusalem—God's unwillingness to make judgment on the city's infidelity the last word that its people would hear. The book makes use of a variety of literary techniques—both prose and poetry—to move people to see that Jerusalem did have a future with God. The book's principal characters—the Holy One of Israel, the virgin daughter Zion, and the Servant of the Lord—engage the reader in a drama of great emotion and intensity. Other personalities appear as the book's reflection on Israel's life with God oscillates between judgment and salvation. These include the prophet Isaiah and his two strangely named sons; King Ahaz and his son Hezekiah; Cyrus the Persian; the owner of an unproductive vineyard; the Assyrian army; the nations; the poor; and Immanuel. Justice for the poor is a theme that continually surfaces throughout the book, leading the reader to conclude that Israel's relationship with its God is indirect—that it is a by-product of the creation and maintenance of a just society.

Those who read this book from beginning to end will experience a range of emotions that testify to the book's complexity. They will sympathize with the prophet's friend who expected to find a good harvest of grapes in his vineyard (Isa 5). They will be in awe with the prophet as he experiences the majesty of God (Isa 6). They will puzzle at the obtuseness of Ahaz (Isa 7). They will reel at the intense hatred of the oracles against the nations (Isa 13–27). They will be relieved as they hear of Jerusalem's liberation (Isa 40). They will be shocked at the suffering of the Servant of the Lord (52:13–53:12). They will be happy for mother Zion embraced by her husband and surrounded by her children again (Isa 62, 66). And they will be disappointed by the book's ending (66:24). The last verse is so depressing that when the final verses of Isaiah are read in the synagogue, by custom the reader repeats verse 23, with its more upbeat tone, after reading verse 24 so that the book does not end on a negative note.

The influence of the book of Isaiah

The book of Isaiah continues to have a profound influence on its readers—especially those who belong to two of the religious traditions that developed from the religion of ancient Israel: Judaism and Christianity. The book of Isaiah is often read in the synagogue as the *Haftarah*, the reading that is meant to parallel and illuminate the reading from the torah. Also, the significance of Jerusalem in the book of Isaiah has helped shaped Judaism's attitude toward this city. Especially significant is the vision of justice and peace with which the city will be blessed (see 2:2-4; 11:6-9).

The Christian confession of Jesus as the Messiah has been shaped significantly by the book of Isaiah. Among the more significant references to Isaiah in the New Testament is Matthew's citation of the Immanuel prophecy (Isa 7:14; Matt 2:23), Luke's use of elements from the fourth Servant Song to explain the necessity of Jesus' suffering and death (e.g., Isa 53:7-9; Luke 33:27; Acts 8:32-33), and the idea of the New Jerusalem in the book of Revelation (Isa 65:18; Rev 21:2). The church's early theologians referred to the book of Isaiah as "the fifth Gospel," because they discerned the significance of this book for the New Testament, which cites Isaiah more often than any book of the Hebrew Bible except the book of Psalms.

Isaiah continues to exercise its influence in the church. Passages from Isaiah are read frequently in both the Sunday and weekday lectionaries. The Second Vatican Council cited Isaiah 2:4 and 32:17 in its Constitution on the Church in the Modern World when speaking on social justice and peace (*Gaudium et spes*, 70). Finally, the book's vision for the future has provided liberation theologians with a biblical foundation for their advocacy on behalf of the poor and oppressed.

Composition, structure, and content

Modern scholarly interpretation of Isaiah has been shaped by the recognition that the book is a composite work that reflects three different periods of Jerusalem's history. Chapters 1–23 and 28–39 contain material relating to the ministry of the eighth-century prophet, Isaiah, son of Amoz (1:1-2). He condemned the social, political, and economic system of the kingdom of Judah because it created a two-tiered society made up of the very rich and the very poor. The rich acquired and maintained their position in Judahite society by taking advantage of the poor. What was even worse was that the temple and its liturgy were used to assure the oppressors that God would continue to protect Judah despite its manifest failure to maintain a community of justice. The prophet believed that the aggressively militaristic Assyrian Empire was God's instrument of judgment on the kingdom of Judah. Chapters 36–39 are taken for the most part from 2 Kings 18:13–20:19, which describes the Assyrian siege of Jerusalem.

Isaiah 40–55 (covered in *Isaiah, Part Two*) are the product of an anonymous prophet whose ministry took place about 125 years after that of Isaiah, son of Amoz. The message of these chapters is that there is a future for Jerusalem beyond the disaster that occurred when Nebuchadnezzar, king of Babylon, captured Jerusalem, destroyed the temple, ended the Judahite monarchy and national state, and led off many leading citizens into exile. The rise of Cyrus, the Persian, convinced the anonymous prophet of the exile that Judah's time of judgment was over and that Cyrus was God's chosen instrument to rebuild Jerusalem and its temple (Isa 45). The prophet's exquisite poems helped the people of Judah to make sense of the disaster they experienced and to see that there was a future beyond judgment.

Isaiah 56–66 (covered in *Isaiah, Part Two*) are a collection of poems that reflected the disillusionment of some when the hopes engendered by Isaiah 40–55 did not materialize. While the temple had been rebuilt, the national state was not restored, the economy was in shambles, and the conflict between the wealthy and the poor resurfaced. Despite the disappointment, the poems of chapters 56–66 expect a full and glorious restoration for Judah (Isa 60).

The final component of Isaiah is found in chapters 24–27. These chapters look forward to a day of judgment when God will finally defeat the powers of evil, vindicate the just, and punish evildoers. The day of judgment will end with all God's people, scattered about the world, returning to worship God in Jerusalem (Isa 27:13).

The circumstances under which the book of Isaiah took the form it now has are not entirely clear. Three fairly complete copies of the book of Isaiah were found among the Dead Sea Scrolls, so the book in its present form existed prior to the second century B.C., when the community that produced the scrolls settled near the Dead Sea. The latest components of the book (chaps. 24–27) probably date from no later than the fourth century. More precision than this is not possible at present. The book of Isaiah, then, took the form it now has sometime between the fourth and the second centuries B.C., though the earliest components of the book come from the eighth century B.C.

What is clear is the book's purpose: to give the people of Judah and Jerusalem hope for the future and the will to re-embrace their ancestral religious traditions. Of course, there were other similar attempts. For example, the Deuteronomic tradition tries to persuade Judah that its future is tied up with careful observance of the norms of traditional Israelite morality as articulated in the book of Deuteronomy. The Chronicler asserts that Judah's future depends upon the legitimacy of its temple rituals as marked by their continuity with preexilic liturgical traditions. The book of Isaiah sees Jerusalem's future as God's "creative redemption." Jerusalem's response to this new act of God is to create and maintain a society based on justice and equity.

Our approach and major themes

While this commentary assumes the composite character of the book, it will approach the work as a whole with a literary and theological integrity of its own. The divisions of the book adopted here are not those reflecting the history of its composition but its literary shape.

The book falls into five parts of approximately the same length, which usually begin with an oracle of judgment on pride and arrogance and end with a word of salvation. Each of these sections is addressed to Jerusalem. These five sections are chapters 1–12: Jerusalem's Future; chapters 13–27: Jerusalem and the Nations; chapters 28–39: Judgment and Salvation for Jerusalem (*Isaiah, Part One*); chapters 40–55: Jerusalem's Liberation; and chapters 56–66: The New Jerusalem (*Isaiah, Part Two*).

There are two principal themes that are the literary and theological linchpins of the book of Isaiah. The first flows from the distinctive title the book of Isaiah gives for God: "the Holy One of Israel." This unique Isaianic way of speaking about Jerusalem's God was formulated to expand the people's notion of deity. The Lord was unlike any other god and did not act as Jerusalem expected God to act. The holiness of God, then, was not a "moral" quality. It was God's otherness and singularity. It was manifest in the way God acted toward Jerusalem and the nations. In the first three sections of the book (1–12; 13–27; 28–39), God demands that Jerusalem create and maintain a society based on justice. The consequence for failing to do this will be severe judgment, including the loss of the state, dynasty, temple, and land. In the fourth section of the book (40–55), there are several instances when "Holy One" is followed by the term "redeemer" (41:14; 43:14; 47:4; 48:17). In the last section, the nations will recognize the holiness of Israel's God because of Jerusalem's commitment to justice (57:15; 60:9, 14).

The second principal theme of the book is Jerusalem/Zion. The portrait that the prophet paints of the city contrasts sharply with that of the "Holy One of Israel." While the Lord demands justice for the poor, Jerusalem and its leaders crush them. While God's holiness has been made known to Israel throughout its history, Jerusalem seeks its security in alliances with other nations and through the worship of other gods. When God declares that Jerusalem has paid for its sins, the people are hesitant to believe. Despite this, God never stops loving Jerusalem and its people. God is determined to provide Jerusalem with a glorious future. The interaction between the Holy One of Israel and Jerusalem is the engine that drives Isaiah.

To appreciate the book's achievement, it is best to read the text straight through first without the commentary, if possible. This will allow the reader to get a sense of the book as a whole. Such a sustained reading will evoke from the reader a variety of responses. Reading the commentary then will help the reader probe more deeply into parts of the text that are particularly intriguing, inspiring, or puzzling. The most creative interaction with the text will result from the reader's recognition that the book is an expression of faith—faith in the Holy One of Israel and in the future of Jerusalem. The book is confident that judgment, though deserved by the city, is never God's last word to Jerusalem. The Jewish reader still looks to the final redemption of Jerusalem, while the book's Christian reader looks for the coming of the new and heavenly Jerusalem. The faith of both has been shaped decisively by the book of Isaiah.

JERUSALEM'S FUTURE

Isaiah 1:1–12:6

The first section of the book of Isaiah begins with an indictment of Jerusalem's infidelity (1:2-9) and ends with a prayer of thanksgiving for its restoration in the future (12:1-6). Between these two poles, Isaiah alternates between harsh and explicit descriptions of the judgment that awaits Jerusalem for its role in creating an unjust society, and lyrical and touching images of the future beyond judgment that God has for the city and its people. The genius of the prophet was not only his ability to appreciate the realities of the political and military crises in Jerusalem's immediate future but especially his ability to see beyond these to a glorious future for Zion. Still, Isaiah was no Pollyanna as his words make clear. He was certain that Jerusalem was to undergo a severe crisis that included political impotence and military defeat. Even more devastating would be the loss of and exile from the land that God promised to ancient Israel's ancestors. But beyond this judgment on Jerusalem was the promise of a new city ruled by a good king who led a people committed to justice.

1:1 The prophet's name

The book identifies itself as the "vision" of Isaiah. It is a vision—the prophet's dream—of

I. Isaiah 1–39

CHAPTER 1

¹The vision which Isaiah, son of Amoz, saw concerning Judah and Jerusalem in the days of Uzziah, Jotham, Ahaz and Hezekiah, kings of Judah.

Accusation and Appeal

²Hear, O heavens, and listen, O earth,
 for the LORD speaks:
Sons have I raised and reared,
 but they have rebelled against me!
³An ox knows its owner,
 and an ass, its master's manger;
But Israel does not know,
 my people has not understood.
⁴Ah! Sinful nation, people laden with wickedness,
 evil offspring, corrupt children!
They have forsaken the LORD,
 spurned the Holy One of Israel,
 apostatized,
⁵Why would you yet be struck,
 that you continue to rebel?
The whole head is sick,
 the whole heart faint.
⁶From the sole of the foot to the head
 there is no sound spot in it;
Just bruise and welt and oozing wound,
 not drained, or bandaged,
 or eased with salve.

continue

what he imagined Jerusalem's future to be. The prophet's name clarifies that vision. The name "Isaiah" means "the Lord saves." The naming of four Judahite kings asserts that what follows was first proclaimed in the eighth century B.C. when Jerusalem faced severe political, economic, and military crises.

1:2-9 God's judgment

The prophet's words begin with a poignant cry of betrayal. That the prophet identifies God

⁷Your country is waste,
  your cities burnt with fire;
Your land—before your eyes
  strangers devour it,
  a waste, like the devastation of Sodom.
⁸And daughter Zion is left
  like a hut in a vineyard,
Like a shed in a melon patch,
  like a city blockaded.
⁹If the LORD of hosts had not
  left us a small remnant,
We would have become as Sodom,
  would have resembled Gomorrah.

¹⁰Hear the word of the LORD,
  princes of Sodom!
Listen to the instruction of our God,
  people of Gomorrah!
¹¹What do I care for the multitude of your
    sacrifices?
  says the LORD.
I have had enough of whole-burnt rams
  and fat of fatlings;
In the blood of calves, lambs, and goats
  I find no pleasure.
¹²When you come to appear before me,
  who asks these things of you?
¹³Trample my courts no more!
  To bring offerings is useless;
  incense is an abomination to me.
New moon and sabbath, calling assemblies—
  festive convocations with wickedness—
  these I cannot bear.
¹⁴Your new moons and festivals I detest;
  they weigh me down, I tire of the load.
¹⁵When you spread out your hands,
  I will close my eyes to you;
Though you pray the more,
  I will not listen.
Your hands are full of blood!
  ¹⁶Wash yourselves clean!
Put away your misdeeds from before my eyes;
  cease doing evil;
  ¹⁷learn to do good.

continue

as the parent betrayed and Israel as God's guilty children implies that judgment will not be God's last word to Israel. Like the love of parents for their children, God's love for Israel does not fail because of Israel's failures. The second comparison, likening Israel with beasts of burden, suggests that Israel acted out of ignorance, not appreciating the nature of its relationship with God. This also suggests some mitigation of Israel's guilt. Still, this will not prevent Israel from experiencing God's judgment for its infidelity. What the prophet cannot understand is the reason Israel has not learned from experience. Its infidelity continued until its cities were destroyed, its land desolate, and Jerusalem abandoned. Still, God did not allow Israel to destroy itself, but kept a few survivors alive. These survivors have accepted their situation as the Lord's doing, and they recognize the miracle that God worked in keeping them alive.

In verse 9, the prophet introduces what will be a significant theme in the book: the remnant. The survival of the "small remnant" prevented Jerusalem and the other cities of Judah from sharing the fate of Sodom and Gomorrah (see Gen 19:24-25). Paul quotes verse 9 in the course of his impassioned discourse on God's continuing love for the Jewish people (Rom 9:27-29).

1:10-20 Israel's worship

Taking on the persona of God, the prophet picks up on the reference to Sodom and Gomorrah in verse 9 to introduce a critique of Israel's liturgy that has few parallels in comprehensiveness and intensity. God rejects Israel's religious festivals, sacrifices, and acts of personal piety because Israel has not maintained a just society. Without justice, Israel's worship of the Lord is an empty shell. The book of Isaiah ends with another stinging critique of ritual activity (66:1-4). The book, then, is framed by bitter and comprehensive criticisms of ritual because the prophet believed Israel's communal worship facilitated its selective obedience. Israel believed that God must be pleased with it because of its liturgy even though its social, political, and economic life was a mockery of justice.

Still, God's judgment is not final because God asks Israel to consider what it has done. Israel has to choose between life and death. Obedience is not a matter of knowledge. It is a matter of will. If Israel chooses to live in obedience, then red can become white. Sin can be countered by repentance.

 Isaiah's **criticism of Israel's liturgical practice** (1:11-17), while unique in the forceful way it is expressed, does have parallels elsewhere in Scripture. Similar sentiments are voiced by other prophets (Jer 6:20; Hos 6:6; Mic 6:7-8), as well as in Wisdom literature (Sir 34:23) and Psalms (50:7-13). In the Gospel of Matthew, Jesus also rejects mere formalism in religious rituals, reminding his listeners on more than one occasion that what God truly desires is "mercy, not sacrifice" (Matt 9:13; 12:7).

To put the apocalyptic vision recorded in the book of Revelation into words, John studied the book of Isaiah. In describing the devastation of Jerusalem at the end of the age, John alludes to verse 10 and the application of the name Sodom to Jerusalem (Rev 11:8). As a book of prophecy, Isaiah assumes that the people of Judah are in control of their future: the choices *they* make will create their future. The prophet's task is to help the people appreciate the consequences of their choices. Because they have created a society based on injustice and oppression, that society will collapse. The book also affirms that judgment will not be the last word that God will address to Judah. God will restore Jerusalem, giving the people another opportunity to create a just society in which all will enjoy God's peace.

The book of Revelation is an example of an apocalyptic worldview that does not envision the triumph of divine justice in *this* world. Apocalyptic looks forward to a new world to be created by the power of God. The climax of the book of Revelation occurs in chapter 21 with

Make justice your aim: redress the wronged, hear the orphan's plea, defend the widow.

¹⁸Come now, let us set things right, says the LORD:
Though your sins be like scarlet, they may become white as snow;
Though they be red like crimson, they may become white as wool.
¹⁹If you are willing, and obey, you shall eat the good things of the land;
²⁰But if you refuse and resist, you shall be eaten by the sword:
for the mouth of the LORD has spoken!

continue

Isaiah, Engraving by Gustave Dore

its vision of a *"new* heaven and a *new* earth" (Rev 21:1; emphasis added). But like the book of Isaiah, Revelation identifies Jerusalem as the focal point of the new earth (Rev 21:9-27).

19

The Purification of Jerusalem

²¹How she has become a prostitute,
   the faithful city, so upright!
Justice used to lodge within her,
   but now, murderers.
²²Your silver is turned to dross,
   your wine is mixed with water.
²³Your princes are rebels
   and comrades of thieves;
Each one of them loves a bribe
   and looks for gifts.
The fatherless they do not defend,
   the widow's plea does not reach them.
²⁴Now, therefore, says the Lord,
   the LORD of hosts, the Mighty One of
      Israel:
Ah! I will take vengeance on my foes
   and fully repay my enemies!
²⁵I will turn my hand against you,
   and refine your dross in the furnace,
      removing all your alloy.
²⁶I will restore your judges as at first,
   and your counselors as in the beginning;
After that you shall be called
   city of justice, faithful city.
²⁷Zion shall be redeemed by justice,
   and her repentant ones by righteousness.
²⁸Rebels and sinners together shall be crushed,
   those who desert the LORD shall be
      consumed.

Judgment on the Sacred Groves

²⁹You shall be ashamed of the terebinths
   which you desired,
and blush on account of the gardens
   which you chose.
³⁰You shall become like a terebinth whose
   leaves wither,
like a garden that has no water.
³¹The strong tree shall turn to tinder,
   and the one who tends it shall become a
      spark;
Both of them shall burn together,
   and there shall be none to quench them.

continue

1:21-28 Jerusalem's future

At one time, Jerusalem's social and economic system was just. What once was, however, is no more, and the city faces divine judgment. Its political leadership is venal (1:26). The city's leaders should have been protecting the economically vulnerable, but they have used their position to exploit the poor to enrich themselves and thereby have become God's enemies. However, the goal of God's judgment against Jerusalem's elite is not mere vengeance, but the elimination of the city's corrupt political system. With new leadership, Jerusalem can once again be a just and faithful city. Still, the prophet is clear that Zion's current leadership provoked the divine judgment that was coming on Jerusalem. But one day God will provide the city with leaders who have a measure of integrity. The prophet insists that Jerusalem's standing before God is not a consequence of its unique status as the dwelling place of God on earth. Jerusalem's salvation lies in the doing of justice. The city's fate then will be a consequence of its people's commitment to maintaining a just and equitable economic system that protects the most vulnerable people. The future of Jerusalem is in the hands of its people and leaders.

Isaiah's use of **the refining of metals** (1:25) as an image for God's purification of the corrupt is a common symbol in the Old Testament (e.g., Ps 66:10; Prov 25:4-5; Mal 3:2).

1:29-31 False worship

These verses are likely veiled references to the worship of the goddess Asherah, whose rituals may have involved trees in some way (see Jer 17:2). Asherah was the wife of El, the supreme deity of the Ugaritic pantheon. An inscription found on the Sinai Peninsula suggests that some worshipers of the Lord honored Asherah as the Lord's consort. The prophet objects to worship related to Asherah explicitly in 17:8 and 27:9, and the third part of the book (40–55) is filled with parodies of idol worship. Such worship provided ideological support for an unjust social system based on an elite who controlled the economic lives of the poor. The Lord, however, is a God who takes the side of the poor against those who exploit them.

2:1-4 Jerusalem of the future

The prophet speaks not of the Jerusalem of his day but of Jerusalem in the distant future—a time after the city is purged by the coming judgment. Isaiah is convinced that the city's status will change in the future. However, that status will not be the consequence of God's presence in the temple, but of the city's role as the place to which all peoples will come to learn the torah. The prophet does not speak of the nations as enemies to be defeated but as peoples with whom Judah is to live in peace. The enemy that will be defeated is war. The universal observance of the torah will bring an era of peace. The fourth and fifth sections of the book (40–55; 56–66) develop the themes of the future of Jerusalem and Israel's relations with other peoples.

A variation of this oracle occurs in Micah 4:1-4, while Joel 4:10 turns the oracle's imagery inside out. The book of Isaiah returns to the imagery and thought of 2:1-4 several times, e.g., 5:25; 9:6; 11:6-9; 30:27-28; 51:4; 56:6-8; 60:11-14. These passages underscore the book's purpose of helping its readers appreciate what God has in store for Jerusalem.

2:5-22 The day of judgment

The refrain "the LORD alone will be exalted on that day" (2:11 and 17) sets the tone of this poem on the subject of what lies ahead for Jerusalem. Judgment is coming because of divination, Judah's "prosperity," and idolatry (2:5-11). The Bible is clear about divination: it is forbidden to Israel (Exod 22:17; Lev 20:27; Deut 18:10-11). The reason for this prohibition is that an unfavorable prediction was followed by the use of prayers and rituals to induce the gods to change the fate of those who have received an unfavorable omen. Judah cannot

CHAPTER 2

¹This is what Isaiah, son of Amoz, saw concerning Judah and Jerusalem.

Zion, the Royal City of God

²In days to come,
The mountain of the LORD's house
    shall be established as the highest mountain
    and raised above the hills.
All nations shall stream toward it.
    ³Many peoples shall come and say:
"Come, let us go up to the LORD's mountain,
    to the house of the God of Jacob,
That he may instruct us in his ways,
    and we may walk in his paths."
For from Zion shall go forth instruction,
    and the word of the LORD from Jerusalem.
⁴He shall judge between the nations,
    and set terms for many peoples.
They shall beat their swords into plowshares
    and their spears into pruning hooks;
One nation shall not raise the sword against another,
    nor shall they train for war again.
⁵House of Jacob, come,
    let us walk in the light of the LORD!

The Lord's Day of Judgment on Pride

⁶You have abandoned your people,
    the house of Jacob!
Because they are filled with diviners,
    and soothsayers, like the Philistines;
    with foreigners they clasp hands.
⁷Their land is full of silver and gold,
    there is no end to their treasures;
Their land is full of horses,
    there is no end to their chariots.
⁸Their land is full of idols;
    they bow down to the works of their hands,
    what their fingers have made.
⁹So all shall be abased,
    each one brought low.

continue

Do not pardon them!
¹⁰Get behind the rocks,
    hide in the dust,
From the terror of the LORD
    and the splendor of his majesty!
¹¹The eyes of human pride shall be lowered,
    the arrogance of mortals shall be abased,
    and the LORD alone will be exalted, on
        that day.
¹²For the LORD of hosts will have his day
    against all that is proud and arrogant,
    against all that is high, and it will be
        brought low;
¹³Yes, against all the cedars of Lebanon
    and against all the oaks of Bashan,
¹⁴Against all the lofty mountains
    and all the high hills,
¹⁵Against every lofty tower
    and every fortified wall,
¹⁶Against all the ships of Tarshish
    and all stately vessels.
¹⁷Then human pride shall be abased,
    the arrogance of mortals brought low,
And the LORD alone will be exalted on that
        day.
¹⁸The idols will vanish completely.
¹⁹People will go into caves in the rocks
    and into holes in the earth,
At the terror of the LORD
    and the splendor of his majesty,
    as he rises to overawe the earth.
²⁰On that day people shall throw to moles
        and bats
    their idols of silver and their idols of gold
    which they made for themselves to
        worship.
²¹And they shall go into caverns in the rocks
    and into crevices in the cliffs,
At the terror of the LORD
    and the splendor of his majesty,
    as he rises to overawe the earth.
²²As for you, stop worrying about mortals,
    in whose nostrils is but a breath;
    for of what worth are they?

continue

evade the judgment that is coming on it no matter what rituals may be used to deflect God's will for Israel's immediate future. The country's prosperity benefited the few people at the top of the social and economic hierarchy. The prophet condemned this "prosperity" because it was achieved at the expense of the poor. The worship of gods other than the Lord provided religious support for an unjust social and economic system.

The motif of "the day of the Lord" (2:12) appears frequently in the prophetic tradition (Isa 13:6; Amos 5:18-20; Jer 17:16-18; Ezek 30:3; Joel 1:15). That day was to witness God's final victory over every enemy. What the prophet asserts here is that Israel is among those who will experience God's judgment because of the injustice that the poor must endure. God's ultimate triumph will lead people to cease serving other deities as they finally recognize that Yahweh alone deserves their exclusive service. In describing the terrors of "the day of the Lord," the prophet asserts three times that people will hide themselves among caves and rocks in the attempt to escape judgment (2:10, 19, 21). The book of Revelation uses that same imagery in speaking of the terrors that it sees as coming at the end of the age (Rev 6:15).

Some exegetes interpret the phrase **"with foreigners they clasp hands"** (2:6) as referring to the intermarriage of Israelites with nonbelievers from neighboring lands. Such marriages were forbidden by Mosaic law (Deut 7:2-5) and condemned elsewhere in the Old Testament (see, for example, Neh 13:23-27). Whether the phrase refers to marriage or simply to commercial enterprises or political treaties with foreigners, the purpose of the prohibition is clear: such entanglements always carry with them the danger of introducing idolatrous practices among the people of God.

Ancient Jerusalem

3:1-12 The collapse of the political order

The exaltation of the Lord means the collapse of Jerusalem's political order. The country's leaders will be unable to insure that people have the basic necessities for life: bread and water. One consequence will be the breakdown of society's basic structure. Judah will be without competent leaders. This will result in serious and destructive social conflict. The ensuing situation will be so bad that no one will want to accept a position of leadership.

The prophet makes it clear that the cause of this anarchy was the failure of Judah's leaders to maintain a just society. While there were individuals who conducted their affairs with justice, the society as a whole was a distortion of what God wanted Judah to become. While the just can expect to survive the coming judgment, God means to remake Judahite society by eliminating those responsible for its corruption. In particular, Jerusalem's leaders bear the primary responsibility for the chaos that gripped Judah.

Among the leaders of Judaean society listed in Isaiah 3:1-3, the **"captain of fifty"** refers to a military commander who had charge of fifty men (see also Exod 18:21, 25). The term resembles the Roman military title of "centurion" (who commanded one hundred men).

CHAPTER 3

Judgment on Jerusalem and Judah

¹The Lord, the LORD of hosts,
   will take away from Jerusalem and from
      Judah
Support and staff—
   all support of bread,
   all support of water:
²Hero and warrior,
   judge and prophet, diviner and elder,
³The captain of fifty and the nobleman,
   counselor, skilled magician, and expert
      charmer.
⁴I will place boys as their princes;
   the fickle will govern them,
⁵And the people will oppress one another,
   yes, each one the neighbor.
The child will be insolent toward the elder,
   and the base toward the honorable.
⁶When anyone seizes a brother
   in their father's house, saying,
"You have clothes! Be our ruler,
   and take in hand this ruin!"—
⁷He will cry out in that day:
"I cannot be a healer,
   when there is neither bread nor clothing
      in my own house!
   You will not make me a ruler of the people!"
⁸Jerusalem has stumbled, Judah has fallen;
   for their speech and deeds affront the
      LORD,
   a provocation in the sight of his majesty.
⁹Their very look bears witness against them;
   they boast of their sin like Sodom,
They do not hide it.
   Woe to them!
   They deal out evil to themselves.
¹⁰Happy the just, for it will go well with them,
   the fruit of their works they will eat.
¹¹Woe to the wicked! It will go ill with them,
   with the work of their hands they will be
      repaid.
¹²My people—infants oppress them,
   women rule over them!

continue

My people, your leaders deceive you,
  they confuse the paths you should follow.

¹³The LORD rises to accuse,
  stands to try his people.
¹⁴The Lord enters into judgment
  with the people's elders and princes:
You, you who have devoured the vineyard;
  the loot wrested from the poor is in your
    houses.
¹⁵What do you mean by crushing my people,
  and grinding down the faces of the poor?
says the Lord, the GOD of hosts.

The Haughty Women of Zion

¹⁶The LORD said:
  Because the daughters of Zion are haughty,
  and walk with necks outstretched,
Ogling and mincing as they go,
  their anklets tinkling with every step,
¹⁷The Lord shall cover the scalps of Zion's
    daughters with scabs,
  and the LORD shall lay bare their heads.

¹⁸On that day the LORD will do away with the
finery of the anklets, sunbursts, and crescents;
¹⁹the pendants, bracelets, and veils; ²⁰the head-
dresses, bangles, cinctures, perfume boxes, and
amulets; ²¹the signet rings, and the nose rings;
²²the court dresses, wraps, cloaks, and purses; ²³the
lace gowns, linen tunics, turbans, and shawls.

²⁴Instead of perfume there will be stench,
  instead of a girdle, a rope,
And instead of elaborate coiffure, baldness;
  instead of a rich gown, a sackcloth skirt.
Then, instead of beauty, shame.
²⁵Your men will fall by the sword,
  and your champions, in war;
²⁶Her gates will lament and mourn,
  as the city sits desolate on the ground.

CHAPTER 4

¹Seven women will take hold of one man
  on that day, saying:

continue

3:13–4:1 Judgment upon the wealthy

The prophet was convinced that the fall of
Judah and Jerusalem was the inevitable consequence of decisions made by the people of
means. To demonstrate their responsibility, the
prophet pictures them on trial before God, who
accuses them of oppressing the poor. The
prophet singles out rich women flaunting their
wealth for all to see. When judgment comes,
God will destroy every single bit of finery with
which these women flaunt the prosperity
gained at the expense of the poor. The rich have
stolen from the poor to give themselves the
best of everything. Judgment is coming and
they will lose everything. The rich will then
learn what it means to be poor. War will rob
Judah of its young people and plunge it into
mourning. Judah's losses in war will turn its
women into widows who will contend with
one another for the chance to marry the few
remaining men.

Isaiah and Israel's other prophets
repeatedly stressed **society's
responsibility to care for the poor and
vulnerable**. The U.S. bishops, in their
pastoral letter *Economic Justice for All*
(1986), remind us: "As followers of Christ,
we are challenged to make a fundamental
'option for the poor'—to speak for the
voiceless, to defend the defenseless, to
assess lifestyles, policies, and social
institutions in terms of their impact on the
poor. . . . As Christians we are called to
respond to the needs of all our brothers
and sisters, but those with the greatest
needs require the greatest response" (16).

4:2-6 Jerusalem's restoration

Though the prophet warns Jerusalem of the
judgment that is coming upon it, he never
claims that judgment is God's last word to the
city. On the contrary, Isaiah was able to see beyond the immediate crisis. Of course, the corruption of the city's leadership and the idleness
of its wealthy class evoke a purifying visitation

from God. Still, the prophet envisions a new city, one that God will create following the terrible judgment that is coming on an economy founded on injustice toward the poor. What the immediate future holds for Jerusalem is the purging that will come with "searing judgment," leaving only a remnant in the city. God will protect those who survive this judgment and then refound Zion.

The temple does not appear to have a significant place in the prophet's vision of a new Jerusalem. Isaiah envisions the Zion of the future with God present not in some grandiose structure but in the humble shelter of the peasant farmer. The judgment that is coming on Jerusalem is not vindictiveness but has as its purpose the preparation of the purified remnant. This remnant will witness God's reestablishment of the city on the basis of justice and equity. While Isaiah condemns the Jerusalem of his day because of its exploitive social and economic system, he sees a new Jerusalem cleansed of the sins of its past.

"We will eat our own food
and wear our own clothing;
Only let your name be given us,
put an end to our disgrace!"

Jerusalem Purified

²On that day,
The branch of the LORD will be beauty and
glory,
and the fruit of the land will be honor
and splendor
for the survivors of Israel.
³Everyone who remains in Zion,
everyone left in Jerusalem
Will be called holy:
everyone inscribed for life in Jerusalem.
⁴When the Lord washes away
the filth of the daughters of Zion,
And purges Jerusalem's blood from her midst
with a blast of judgment, a searing blast,
⁵Then will the LORD create,
over the whole site of Mount Zion
and over her place of assembly,
A smoking cloud by day
and a light of flaming fire by night.
⁶For over all, his glory will be shelter and
protection:
shade from the parching heat of day,
refuge and cover from storm and rain.

 Clouds and Smoke

The "smoking cloud" that Isaiah envisions God creating over Mount Zion after the purification of Jerusalem (4:5) recalls the "column of cloud" that guided the Israelites during their flight from Egypt (Exod 13:21). In the Old Testament, smoking clouds are often a sign of God's presence and an emblem of God's glory. When God came down upon Mount Sinai, for example, the mountain "was completely enveloped in smoke," and a column of cloud descended at the entrance of the tent of meeting when God came to speak to Moses (Exod 19:18; 33:9; 40:34). A cloud also filled the inner sanctuary of the temple built by Solomon as a sign that God had made the temple a divine dwelling place (1 Kgs 8:10-13). Even God's heavenly throne was imagined as being enveloped in "cloud and darkness" (Ps 97:2). Isaiah will also encounter clouds (or "smoke") as a symbol of God's presence during his call to prophecy in 6:4.

Lesson One

EXPLORING LESSON ONE

1. According to the Introduction, why did the early theologians of the church refer to Isaiah as "the fifth Gospel"?

_____

_____

_____

_____

_____

2. What does the Introduction say is the clear purpose of the book of Isaiah?

_____

_____

_____

_____

_____

3. What do the prophet's opening words concerning Israel's betrayal tell us about the nature of God's relationship with Israel (1:2)? (See 49:15; 64:7; Jer 31:9; Hos 11:1.)

_____

_____

_____

_____

_____

4. a) Why is God rejecting Judah's temple worship (1:10-17)? (See Jer 7:4-5; Hos 6:4-6; Matt 9:13.)

_____

_____

_____

_____

b) In what way can Isaiah's message be applied to our own liturgical life today?

_____

_____

_____

_____

5. Despite Israel's sinfulness, God urges the people to repent and receive the cleansing gift of forgiveness (1:18). How have you experienced God's offer of compassion and healing in your own life?

_____

_____

_____

_____

_____

6. What specific conditions in Judah's society are bringing it into God's judgment (1:22-25)? (See Deut 16:19-20.)

_____

_____

_____

_____

_____

7. What does the text of 2:12-17, which strongly emphasizes God's judgment, have in common with Mary's song (the *Magnificat*) in Luke 1:46-55?

_____

_____

_____

_____

_____

8. a) What signs of social chaos found in 3:1-9 also afflict societies today? (See Mal 3:23-24.)

_____

_____

_____

_____

b) In what ways has your faith helped you to find order in an unsettled world?

_____

_____

_____

_____

9. A major shift in focus occurs between 4:1 and 4:2. What does this shift say about God's ultimate intentions for God's people?

_____

_____

_____

_____

_____

10. What memories would Isaiah's promise of "a smoking cloud by day / and a light of flaming fire by night" (4:5) stir up in the people of Judah? (See Exod 13:21.)

_____

_____

_____

_____

_____

CLOSING PRAYER

Prayer

Come now, let us set things right,
  says the LORD:
Though your sins be like scarlet,
  they may become white as snow;
Though they be red like crimson,
  they may become white as wool. (Isa 1:18)

We acknowledge our failings, Lord, but help us not to be overly discouraged or dismayed by them. Instead, fill us with joyful hope at the promise of redemption proclaimed by your prophet, and let us begin to transform our lives this very day, forsaking any path that leads us away from you. Help us to seek and to find you today, especially through . . .

LESSON TWO

Isaiah 5–11

Begin your personal study and group discussion with a simple and sincere prayer such as:

Prayer

Heavenly Father, as we read the words of your prophet Isaiah, help us respond to his call to repentance and a new way of life. May our study inspire us to imitate you, the pillar of justice and the fountain of all mercy.

Read the Bible text of Isaiah 5–11 found in the outside columns of pages 30–45, highlighting what stands out to you.

Read the accompanying commentary to add to your understanding.

Respond to the questions on pages 46–48, Exploring Lesson Two.

The Closing Prayer on page 48 is for your personal use and may be used at the end of group discussion.

CHAPTER 5

The Song of the Vineyard

¹Now let me sing of my friend,
my beloved's song about his vineyard.
My friend had a vineyard
on a fertile hillside;
²He spaded it, cleared it of stones,
and planted the choicest vines;
Within it he built a watchtower,
and hewed out a wine press.
Then he waited for the crop of grapes,
but it yielded rotten grapes.
³Now, inhabitants of Jerusalem, people of
Judah,
judge between me and my vineyard:
⁴What more could be done for my vineyard
that I did not do?
Why, when I waited for the crop of grapes,
did it yield rotten grapes?
⁵Now, I will let you know
what I am going to do to my vineyard:
Take away its hedge, give it to grazing,
break through its wall, let it be trampled!
⁶Yes, I will make it a ruin:
it shall not be pruned or hoed,
but will be overgrown with thorns and
briers;
I will command the clouds
not to rain upon it.
⁷The vineyard of the LORD of hosts is the
house of Israel,
the people of Judah, his cherished plant;
He waited for judgment, but see, bloodshed!
for justice, but hark, the outcry!

continue

5:1-7 The song of the vineyard

The prophet returns to words of judgment against Jerusalem and Judah, but this judgment is veiled in an allegory about his "friend's" vineyard (see also Hos 10:1; Jer 2:21; Ezek 19:10-14; Matt 21:33; Mark 12:1; Luke 20:10). The prophet's friend invested time and energy into his vineyard with the expectation of a return on this investment. For crops like grapes, full production did not begin for several years after the vines were planted. The owner of the vineyard had to have confidence and patience that a harvest would come one day. But the song is about disappointment. The anticipated results of the efforts do not materialize: the vineyard produces only bitter grapes. The owner of the vineyard speaks directly to the reader, asking advice because he will have to make a decision about the future of the vineyard soon. The questioning reflects a degree of pathos, since the unspoken answer to the owner's questions is "nothing."

The owner will not tear up the vines and destroy them as one would expect but will rather remove his care and protection from the vineyard. The owner will stop the cultivation of the vineyard and will allow the natural course of events to take place. By tearing down the wall, the owner will open the vineyard to animals that will eat the grapes. Their grazing will put the plants at risk. The owner will not have the vines pruned. They will then grow too long to support the fruit. By failing to hoe, the owner makes it possible for weeds to grow and compete for nutrients and moisture. Eventually, the weeds will dominate the vineyard and the grapevines will become weak and stunted. The prophet implies that divine judgment on Jerusalem is the absence of God's sustaining presence, leaving the city prey to those who will take advantage of its weakness.

The people of Judah have not met God's expectations. They were to be a blessing to the world, i.e., they were to produce fruit. They were to fulfill their calling in the world as the people of God by maintaining a society whose values were shaped by righteousness and justice. The vineyard will be abandoned and without care or cultivation. It will be overrun and eventually destroyed. God will abandon Judah to those who would conquer it.

5:8-23 Judah's crimes

After the allegorical indictment found in the song of the vineyard, the prophet becomes specific. He begins by condemning the large estates of the wealthy (5:8-11). The people of means were able to acquire their large estates by taking advantage of the economic reverses of the poor and confiscating their land for the nonpayment of debts. The wealthy cultivated grapes and olives on their land to increase production of wine and olive oil. The export and sale of these commodities were highly profitable. Because more land was given to the cultivation of crops for export, less land was available for growing grains to feed Judah's people. With less grain available for sale, the price of this staple rose, putting more economic pressure on the poor. This helped create a permanent underclass in Judah. This breach of traditional Israelite morality would bring terrible consequences. The prophet promises that the land will not yield the increase the wealthy were expecting. They will have to face the kind of economic pressures that were part of the daily experience of the poor.

The prophet condemns the extravagant lifestyle of the wealthy (5:11-17). Most Judahite farmers were able to raise enough crops to feed their families and animals, to set aside seed for the next planting, and to have something to offer at the shrines to thank God for the land's fertility. The wealthy lived in excess, but the prophet assures them that they will learn what

Oracles of Reproach

[8]Ah! Those who join house to house,
who connect field with field,
Until no space remains, and you alone dwell
in the midst of the land!
[9]In my hearing the LORD of hosts has sworn:
Many houses shall be in ruins,
houses large and fine, with nobody living there.
[10]Ten acres of vineyard
shall yield but one bath,
And a homer of seed
shall yield but an ephah.
[11]Ah! Those who rise early in the morning
in pursuit of strong drink,
lingering late
inflamed by wine,
[12]Banqueting on wine with harp and lyre,
timbrel and flute,
But the deed of the LORD they do not regard,
the work of his hands they do not see!
[13]Therefore my people go into exile
for lack of understanding,
Its nobles starving,
its masses parched with thirst.
[14]Therefore Sheol enlarges its throat
and opens its mouth beyond measure;
Down into it go nobility and masses,
tumult and revelry.
[15]All shall be abased, each one brought low,
and the eyes of the haughty lowered,
[16]But the LORD of hosts shall be exalted by judgment,
by justice the Holy God shown holy.
[17]Lambs shall graze as at pasture,
young goats shall eat in the ruins of the rich.
[18]Ah! Those who tug at guilt with cords of perversity,
and at sin as if with cart ropes!
[19]Who say, "Let him make haste,
let him speed his work, that we may see it;
On with the plan of the Holy One of Israel!
let it come to pass, that we may know it!"

continue

20 Ah! Those who call evil good, and good
> evil,
>> who change darkness to light, and light
>> into darkness,
>> who change bitter to sweet, and sweet
>> into bitter!
21 Ah! Those who are wise in their own eyes,
>> prudent in their own view!
22 Ah! Those who are champions at drinking
> wine,
>> masters at mixing drink!
23 Those who acquit the guilty for bribes,
>> and deprive the innocent of justice!
24 Therefore, as the tongue of fire licks up
> stubble,
>> as dry grass shrivels in the flame,
> Their root shall rot
>> and their blossom scatter like dust;
> For they have rejected the instruction of the
> LORD of hosts,
>> and scorned the word of the Holy One of
>> Israel.

25 Therefore the wrath of the LORD blazes
>> against his people,
>> he stretches out his hand to strike them;
> The mountains quake,
>> their corpses shall be like refuse in the
>> streets.
> For all this, his wrath is not turned back,
>> his hand is still outstretched.

continue

The word **"root"** assumes different shades of meaning in its various uses throughout Isaiah. In its first appearance (5:24), the term refers to an unseen, underlying cause for an observable behavior. Later in Isaiah, "root" refers to the ancestor from whom the new Davidic king, who will be God's agent for the deliverance of his people, will descend (11:1). Isaiah also uses the term to indicate the re-establishment of God's people on the land following their return from exile: "The remaining survivors of the house of Judah / shall again strike root below / and bear fruit above" (37:31).

it means to live on the subsistence level. The people of means were able to acquire their wealth by ignoring God's will, by perverting the values of traditional Israelite morality, by their conceit, and by bribery (5:18-22). Because they have ignored the torah, which makes God's will for Israel clear, they can expect only the worst. Unable to cope, they will die in record numbers and the poor will be able to reclaim their heritage. God will insure that justice triumphs.

5:24-30 The means of judgment

The divine judgment that Judah will experience is coming. The result will be the destruction of the nation that has injustice as its foundation. The prophet is aware of the expansionist policies of Judah's more powerful neighbors. He sees Judah falling to their military might. What the rich were doing to the poor, Judah's neighbors would shortly do to the nation as a whole. They will destroy a society whose social and economic values are so out of touch with traditional Israelite morality that they deserve the condemnation that the prophet pronounces on them in the name of God.

 The prospect that corpses will lie "like refuse in the streets" (5:25) as a sign of God's wrath would have been extremely disturbing to Isaiah's original audience. **Being deprived of a proper burial** was not only seen as a terrible fate but a sure sign of God's condemnation (see Jer 14:16; 36:30; 1 Kgs 14:10-11). The later book of Tobit serves as a premier biblical example of this belief. Tobit risks his life to bury kindred who have been killed by the Assyrians, a sign of both his personal virtue and the horror with which Jews viewed the absence of funereal rites and burial (Tob 1:17-18; 2:3-8).

6:1-13 The call of the prophet

Judgment upon Judah was necessary and inevitable. The prophet was to have a critical role in making the people of Judah aware of that judgment so that when it did come they would recognize it for what it was: judgment on a society whose values were a perversion of God's will for Israel. There was to be no mistaking what was to befall Judah as the result of the military strength of imperialistic neighbors or any inability of Israel's patron deity to protect it against this imperialism. On the contrary, what was to befall Judah was God's own doing, announced by prophets whom God commissioned to bring Judah God's message of judgment. To dramatize Isaiah's role in this terrible encounter between God and Judah, the tradition describes the "call of Isaiah."

The book supplies a date for this call to remind its readers that Isaiah's ministry took place at a turning point in Judah's history (6:1). The forty-year reign of Uzziah (783–742 B.C.) was over. It had been a time of economic expansion and prosperity, though only a few Judahites enjoyed any economic benefits from the boom times of Uzziah's reign. The peasants

Invasion

²⁶He will raise a signal to a far-off nation,
 and whistle for it from the ends of the earth.
Then speedily and promptly they will come.
²⁷None among them is weary, none stumbles,
 none will slumber, none will sleep.
None with waist belt loose,
 none with sandal thong broken.
²⁸Their arrows are sharp,
 and all their bows are bent,
The hooves of their horses like flint,
 and their chariot wheels like the whirlwind.
²⁹They roar like the lion,
 like young lions, they roar;
They growl and seize the prey,
 they carry it off and none can rescue.
³⁰They will growl over it, on that day,
 like the growling of the sea,
Look to the land—
 darkness closing in,
 the light dark with clouds!

CHAPTER 6

The Sending of Isaiah

¹In the year King Uzziah died, I saw the Lord seated on a high and lofty throne, with the train of his garment filling the temple. ²Seraphim were stationed above; each of them had six wings: with two they covered their faces, with two they covered their feet, and with two they hovered. ³One cried out to the other:

"Holy, holy, holy is the LORD of hosts!
 All the earth is filled with his glory!"

⁴At the sound of that cry, the frame of the door shook and the house was filled with smoke.

⁵Then I said, "Woe is me, I am doomed! For I am a man of unclean lips, living among a people of unclean lips, and my eyes have seen the King, the LORD of hosts!" ⁶Then one of the seraphim flew to me, holding an ember which he had taken with tongs from the altar.

continue

> [7]He touched my mouth with it. "See," he said, "now that this has touched your lips, your wickedness is removed, your sin purged."
>
> [8]Then I heard the voice of the Lord saying, "Whom shall I send? Who will go for us?" "Here I am," I said; "send me!" [9]And he replied: Go and say to this people:
>
> Listen carefully, but do not understand!
> Look intently, but do not perceive!
> [10]Make the heart of this people sluggish,
> dull their ears and close their eyes;
> Lest they see with their eyes, and hear with
> their ears,
> and their heart understand,
> and they turn and be healed.
>
> [11]"How long, O Lord?" I asked. And he replied:
>
> *continue*

were left behind. But Judah's economy would never again be as strong as it was under Uzziah, and the specter of the powerful Assyrian army was on the horizon. Judgment was coming.

The setting for the story of Isaiah's call is in the temple. There the prophet sees God accompanied by seraphim. The name "seraphim" recalls the fiery serpents of the wilderness tradition (Num 21:6-9; Deut 8:15). The Hebrew word "seraphim" means "the burning ones" and was used as the name of snakes whose venom caused a burning sensation in a person bitten by them. According to the story in Numbers and Deuteronomy, God used these serpents to punish the Israelites for their murmuring. The seraphim that the prophet sees are harbingers of what is in store for Judah. Their song underscores the basic affirmation that the book makes: God is holy. This holiness requires the purging of all immorality from those who stand in God's presence. Isaiah recognizes this and believes that he will not survive his encounter with God. It is important to note that the prophet stands in solidarity with his people. He does not see himself as a

morally upright person who has a right to stand in judgment over others, but the seraphs purge the prophet with a burning coal so that he can begin his mission of announcing God's intention to purge Judah.

In postbiblical Jewish tradition and in medieval Christian tradition, the seraphim form a class of angels. While Isaiah 6 presents the seraphim as winged creatures of the heavenly king, it envisions the seraphim as serpents—not angels. During the time of Isaiah, a bronze serpent was still part of the temple's liturgical accouterments. It was destroyed by King Hezekiah (see 2 Kgs 18:4). The loss of that image and the development of angelology led to the inclusion of seraphim among the "nine choirs of angels" in a noncanonical Jewish book known as *The Testament of Adam* (ch. 4). This latter work rather than the biblical text has shaped the image of the seraphim in Christian art.

What is the prophet's mission? The tradition is aware that Isaiah's ministry did not prevent the destruction of the temple, the scattering of its priesthood, the end of the dynasty nor the end of the national state. Experience has shown that the prophet was not called to keep Israel from its destiny but to make Israel aware of that destiny. The prophet's mission was to delay Israel's comprehension of the divine plan until generations later, after Israel's endurance of not one but two devastations of its land and two exiles. These bitter events whose significance is illuminated by the message of the prophet made it impossible for Israel to evade responsibility for its fate.

John, the visionary in the book of Revelation, sees the glory of God and the Lamb just as the prophet Isaiah did (6:2-3; Rev 4:6-8). Matthew cites verses 9-10 to explain the apparent failure of the crowds to respond to Jesus' mission (Matt 13:13-15), while the prophet's words are implicit in both Mark (4:12) and Luke (8:10). Luke has Paul recite this text at the climax of Acts. Rejected by the Jews of Rome, Paul turns to the Gentiles, convinced that they will listen (Acts 28:23-29). At the end of his narrative of Jesus' public ministry, the author of the John's Gospel (not to be confused with the author of Revelation) paraphrases verses 9-10 to explain the failure of Jesus to attract a wide following (John 12:39-41). God tells the prophet Isaiah that his message will fall on deaf ears. People will refuse to see the scenario of their future that the prophet describes. The New Testament sees this as true not only for Isaiah but also for Jesus and Paul.

 The story of Isaiah's **call to the prophetic office** contains many of the same elements found in the call narratives of other prophets in the Old Testament. First there is an encounter with God; then an introductory speech followed by a commission; an objection is raised by the potential prophet; and an answer to the objection is provided. Most call narratives end with the granting of a sign to confirm the prophet's appointment. (See Exod 3:1-12; Jer 1:4-10.)

7:1–8:10 Immanuel—God with us

Again after speaking in generalities, the prophet becomes specific. He just spoke about the purpose of his mission as delaying Judah's comprehension of the divine will until there could be no mistaking the divine intention. Now the prophet describes in detail one instance of that lack of comprehension. The prophet details his encounter with Ahaz, the embattled king of Judah, who was under intense pressure to join a coalition of small national states aligned against the imperial power of Assyria.

The king did not want to be dragged into any military action against Assyria, so he sought Assyria's help in maintaining Judah's independence of action. The prophet recognized that while Ahaz's overtures to Assyria would solve the immediate crisis, their long-term effects would be the opposite of the king's goal of keeping Judah independent. Isaiah advised Ahaz to ignore the threats made against him by the coalition aligned against Assyria since that coalition was certain to fail. The prophet's analysis of the

Until the cities are desolate,
  without inhabitants,
Houses, without people,
  and the land is a desolate waste.
[12]Until the LORD sends the people far away,
  and great is the desolation in the midst of the land.
[13]If there remain a tenth part in it,
  then this in turn shall be laid waste;
As with a terebinth or an oak
  whose trunk remains when its leaves have fallen.
Holy offspring is the trunk.

CHAPTER 7

The Syro-Ephraimite War Crisis in Judah

[1]In the days of Ahaz, king of Judah, son of Jotham, son of Uzziah, Rezin, king of Aram, and Pekah, king of Israel, son of Remaliah, went up to attack Jerusalem, but they were not able to conquer it. [2]When word came to the house of David that Aram had allied itself with Ephraim, the heart of the king and heart of the people trembled, as the trees of the forest tremble in the wind.

[3]Then the LORD said to Isaiah: Go out to meet Ahaz, you and your son Shear-jashub, at the end of the conduit of the upper pool, on the highway to the fuller's field, [4]and say to him: Take care you remain calm and do not fear; do not let your courage fail before these two stumps of smoldering brands, the blazing anger of Rezin and the Arameans and of the son of Remaliah—[5]because Aram, with Ephraim and the son of Remaliah, has planned evil against you. They say, [6]"Let us go up against Judah, tear it apart, make it our own by force, and appoint the son of Tabeel king there."

[7]Thus says the Lord GOD:
  It shall not stand, it shall not be!
[8]The head of Aram is Damascus,
  and the head of Damascus is Rezin;
[9]The head of Ephraim is Samaria,
  and the head of Samaria is the son of Remaliah.

continue

Within sixty-five years,
Ephraim shall be crushed, no longer a
nation.
Unless your faith is firm,
you shall not be firm!

Emmanuel

¹⁰Again the LORD spoke to Ahaz: ¹¹Ask for a sign from the LORD, your God; let it be deep as Sheol, or high as the sky! ¹²But Ahaz answered, "I will not ask! I will not tempt the LORD!" ¹³Then he said: Listen, house of David! Is it not enough that you weary human beings? Must you also weary my God? ¹⁴Therefore the Lord himself will give you a sign; the young woman, pregnant and about to bear a son, shall name him Emmanuel. ¹⁵Curds and honey he will eat so that he may learn to reject evil and choose good; ¹⁶for before the child learns to reject evil and choose good, the land of those two kings whom you dread shall be deserted.

¹⁷The LORD shall bring upon you and your people and your father's house such days as have not come since Ephraim seceded from Judah (the king of Assyria). ¹⁸On that day

The LORD shall whistle
    for the fly in the farthest streams of Egypt,
    and for the bee in the land of Assyria.
¹⁹All of them shall come and settle
    in the steep ravines and in the rocky clefts,
    on all thornbushes and in all pastures.

²⁰On that day the Lord shall shave with the razor hired from across the River (the king of Assyria) the head, and the hair of the feet; it shall also shave off the beard. ²¹On that day a man shall keep alive a young cow or a couple of sheep, ²²and from their abundant

continue

passage is the threefold repetition of the Hebrew phrase *immanu el*, which means "God is with us." God is with Judah, but before Judah can experience the saving power of God, it must experience God's judgment on its unjust social and economic system.

This passage is built around several word plays. The first involves the names of Isaiah's sons. God instructed the prophet to take his son and confront Ahaz (7:3). This son's name was *Shear-jashub*, which means "a remnant shall return." The boy's name implies both judgment and salvation for Judah. Only a few of its people will survive the judgment that will involve the end of Judah's political and religious institutions, but God will insure that there will be survivors who will return and begin again. The passage ends with the naming of another of the prophet's sons, *Maher-shalal-hash-baz*, which means "The spoil speeds, the prey hastens." The son who bears this unwieldy name is a living assurance to Ahaz that his fear of the coalition threatening him is baseless. That coalition will collapse before the child learns to say his first words (8:3-4).

Another wordplay occurs as the prophet concludes his words of assurance to Ahaz in verses 7b-9. One way to preserve that wordplay in English translation is to render verse 9b: "If you do not make yourself *firm* (in the Lord), you will not be *affirmed* (by the Lord)." Note the words for firm/affirmed are forms of the Hebrew root *'mn*, which we know from the word "Amen." The prophet asserts that Ahaz need do nothing to save Judah but have confidence in God's words of assurance. With this confidence, Ahaz's own attempts to find security will come to nothing. But Ahaz felt that he had to do something. He was unwilling to accept the prophet's assurances that the Lord was going to protect Judah. A literal translation of Isaiah 65:16 identifies the Lord as "the God of Amen," i.e., the God of assurance, and Revelation 3:14 identifies Jesus as "The Amen."

The most important of the wordplays in this passage are those involving the Hebrew phrase *immanu el*, which occurs three times: 7:14; 8:8, 10. The prophet attempts to support

political situation was more astute than that of Ahaz. But the king could not see it nor could he accept the prophet's advice. This he was fated to do (see 6:9-10) since God's goal was the destruction of the Judahite state because of its injustice toward its own citizens. The irony in this

his words of assurance (7:7-9) that those plotting against Judah are just human beings who will not succeed. Because Ahaz is not content with this assurance, the prophet supports them with a "sign." The prophet calls the king's attention to a pregnant woman that both apparently knew. Isaiah asserts that the crisis will pass before the child, who has yet to be born, is weaned. While the identity of the child is not clear, the significance of the sign is. The prophet advises the king to bide his time and the crisis will pass. He urges Ahaz to regard the birth of the child as a sign of God's presence that will protect Judah from external threats. Matthew (1:22-23) cites this text to underscore the significance of Jesus, whom the evangelist believes to be the very presence of God who has come to save Israel.

The second occurrence of *immanu el* in 8:8 is not as reassuring. The presence it signifies is not a saving presence but one that brings judgment. The prophet affirms that the real danger that Judah faces comes not from the nations allied against it but from an unexpected source. Because the prophet's message has been discounted by king and people, Judah will have to face threats from both Assyria and Egypt (7:18-25; 8:5-8). Still, the prophet is convinced that God's last word to Judah will not be judgment but salvation. While Judah will experience God's judgment through the nations, God will not allow that judgment to consume Judah. The Lord will ever be *immanu el* for Judah (8:9-10).

 God promised David that his descendants would inherit his throne and that his kingdom would endure forever (2 Sam 7:12-16). Like David, each of these kings would be anointed (Hebrew, *mashiach*, from which we get the word "messiah"). If Ahaz loses his throne, **messianic succession** (the dynasty of David) is threatened. Isaiah reassures Ahaz that God has not abandoned him or the promise to David. A child will still be named "God is with us" (7:14).

yield of milk he shall eat curds; curds and honey shall be the food of all who are left in the land. [23]On that day every place where there were a thousand vines worth a thousand pieces of silver shall become briers and thorns. [24]One shall have to go there with bow and arrows, for all the country shall be briers and thorns. [25]But as for all the hills which were hoed with a mattock, for fear of briers and thorns you will not go there; they shall become a place for cattle to roam and sheep to trample.

CHAPTER 8

A Son of Isaiah

[1]The LORD said to me: Take a large tablet, and inscribe on it with an ordinary stylus, "belonging to Maher-shalal-hash-baz," [2]and call reliable witnesses for me, Uriah the priest, and Zechariah, son of Jeberechiah.

[3]Then I went to the prophetess and she conceived and bore a son. The LORD said to me: Name him Maher-shalal-hash-baz, [4]for before the child learns to say, "My father, my mother," the wealth of Damascus and the spoils of Samaria shall be carried off by the king of Assyria.

The Choice: The Lord or Assyria

[5]Again the LORD spoke to me:

[6]Because this people has rejected
the waters of Shiloah that flow gently,
And melts with fear at the display of Rezin
and Remaliah's son,
[7]Therefore the Lord is bringing up against them
the waters of the River, great and mighty,
the king of Assyria and all his glory.
It shall rise above all its channels,
and overflow all its banks.
[8]It shall roll on into Judah,
it shall rage and pass on—
up to the neck it shall reach.
But his outspread wings will fill
the width of your land, Emmanuel!
[9]Band together, O peoples, but be shattered!
Give ear, all you distant lands!

continue

Arm yourselves, but be shattered! Arm
yourselves, but be shattered!
¹⁰Form a plan, it shall be thwarted;
make a resolve, it shall not be carried out,
for "With us is God!"

Disciples of Isaiah

¹¹For thus said the LORD—his hand strong upon
me—warning me not to walk in the way of this
people:

¹²Do not call conspiracy what this people
calls conspiracy,
nor fear what they fear, nor feel dread.
¹³But conspire with the LORD of hosts;
he shall be your fear, he shall be your dread.
¹⁴He shall be a snare,
a stone for injury,
A rock for stumbling
to both the houses of Israel,
A trap and a snare
to those who dwell in Jerusalem;
¹⁵And many among them shall stumble;
fallen and broken;
snared and captured.

¹⁶Bind up my testimony, seal the instruction with
my disciples. ¹⁷I will trust in the LORD, who is hiding
his face from the house of Jacob; yes, I will wait for
him. ¹⁸Here am I and the children whom the LORD
has given me: we are signs and portents in Israel from
the LORD of hosts, who dwells on Mount Zion.
¹⁹And when they say to you, "Inquire of ghosts
and soothsayers who chirp and mutter; should
not a people inquire of their gods, consulting the
dead on behalf of the living, ²⁰for instruction and
testimony?" Surely, those who speak like this are
the ones for whom there is no dawn.

²¹He will pass through it hard-pressed and
hungry,
and when hungry, shall become enraged,
and curse king and gods.
He will look upward,
²²and will gaze at the earth,
But will see only distress and darkness,
oppressive gloom,
murky, without light.

8:11-15 The futility of intrigue

To recapitulate the message of 7:1–8:10, the prophet speaks about the folly of the political intrigue that Ahaz used to secure his country's future. Isaiah has clearly and forcefully conveyed God's assurances that Judah has nothing to fear from any perceived military or political threats to its existence. Rather than fearing political powers, Judah ought to fear God. It is God who is the enemy of Judah as long as its social and economic practices exploit and oppress its own citizens. Indeed, Judah will have to face an enemy but it will not be a human one. God has always been present to Israel as a rock of salvation. But because of its moral failures, the Lord will now become a "rock for stumbling" (8:14). Both Romans 9:33 and 1 Peter 2:8 quote this text to describe the failure of some people to accept Jesus as God's final word to Israel.

8:16-22 The book of the prophet

This passage gives us a glimpse into the beginnings of the book of Isaiah. The prophet asks that his supporters keep a record of what he said so that people will come to see the significance of his words. The many people who discounted the prophet's message turned to divination for insights into Judah's future. Isaiah wants his words to be preserved so that when his message is confirmed by events of Judah's future, people will know that prophets rather than diviners convey God's word to God's people. Hebrews 2:13 quotes verses 17-18 in speaking about how Jesus was made perfect through his suffering.

8:23–9:6 From darkness to light

When the prophet envisions the future, he sees beyond the possibilities of the present to an ideal future. Here the prophet looks forward to the day when the two Israelite kingdoms will be united under the rule of a single, glorious ruler from the Davidic dynasty. The prophet begins his ode to Israel's future by mentioning territories in the far north which were among the first threatened by the Assyrians. He describes the rejoicing of the people saved from Assyrian power. The prophet uses several metaphors to describe God's new act of grace for Israel. It will be like the move from light to darkness and like the harvest that brings an end to the threat of hunger and starvation. The joy it brings will be like that of soldiers over the fruits of their victory. It will remind people of the victory of Gideon over the Midianites (Judg 7:15-25)—a victory that came without the need for striking even a single blow. Israel's future will be the result of a similar victory—so complete as to make the donning of warriors' armor no longer necessary.

The prophet's ode to Israel's future continues as he describes the enthronement of the king who will rule over the Israel created by God's new act of grace. This future king will do what Ahaz could not: he will trust in the fidelity and power of the Lord. This king will not need advisors because his faith will guide him wondrously. He will be an authentic representative of God on earth and will bring an all-embracing and a never-ending peace to God's people. His kingdom will be sustained by justice.

Luke 1:78-79 alludes to this text when he has Zechariah speak about what God will do for Israel. Matthew 4:15-16 cites 9:1-2 as he describes the beginning of Jesus' ministry in Galilee—the region where the territories of Zebulon and Naphtali were located.

 Songs for the coronation of a king appear in several places in the Old Testament (Pss 2, 110; Isa 9:5-6; 11:1-9). The "child" in Isaiah 9:5 is a "son of David" who has just become king and is now almost certainly an adult. The new king of Isaiah 11:1-9 is described as a "shoot" from Jesse, David's father. His reign will be characterized by a peace equal to that of paradise. These readings are used in the Advent liturgy and are interpreted by Christians as applying to Jesus.

The Promise of Salvation Under a New Davidic King

²³There is no gloom where there had been distress. Where once he degraded the land of Zebulun and the land of Naphtali, now he has glorified the way of the Sea, the land across the Jordan, Galilee of the Nations.

CHAPTER 9

¹The people who walked in darkness
   have seen a great light;
Upon those who lived in a land of gloom
   a light has shone.
²You have brought them abundant joy
   and great rejoicing;
They rejoice before you as people rejoice at harvest,
   as they exult when dividing the spoils.
³For the yoke that burdened them,
   the pole on their shoulder,
The rod of their taskmaster,
   you have smashed, as on the day of Midian.
⁴For every boot that tramped in battle,
   every cloak rolled in blood,
   will be burned as fuel for fire.
⁵For a child is born to us, a son is given to us;
   upon his shoulder dominion rests.
They name him Wonder-Counselor, God-Hero,
   Father-Forever, Prince of Peace.
⁶His dominion is vast
   and forever peaceful,
Upon David's throne, and over his kingdom,
   which he confirms and sustains
By judgment and justice,
   both now and forever.
The zeal of the Lord of hosts will do this!

Judgment on the Northern Kingdom

⁷The Lord has sent a word against Jacob,
   and it falls upon Israel;
⁸And all the people know it—
   Ephraim and those who dwell in Samaria—

continue

those who say in arrogance and pride of
heart,

⁹"Bricks have fallen,
but we will rebuild with cut stone;
Sycamores have been felled,
but we will replace them with cedars."

¹⁰So the LORD raises up their foes against them
and stirs up their enemies to action—

¹¹Aram from the east and the Philistines
from the west—
they devour Israel with open mouth.
For all this, his wrath is not turned back,
and his hand is still outstretched!

¹²The people do not turn back to the one
who struck them,
nor do they seek the LORD of hosts.

¹³So the LORD cuts off from Israel head and
tail,
palm branch and reed in one day.

¹⁴(The elder and the noble are the head,
the prophet who teaches falsehood is the
tail.)

¹⁵Those who lead this people lead them astray,
and those who are led are swallowed up.

¹⁶That is why the Lord does not spare their
young men,
and their orphans and widows he does
not pity;
For they are totally impious and wicked,
and every mouth speaks folly.
For all this, his wrath is not turned back,
his hand is still outstretched!

¹⁷For wickedness burns like fire,
devouring brier and thorn;
It kindles the forest thickets,
which go up in columns of smoke.

¹⁸At the wrath of the LORD of hosts the land
quakes,
and the people are like fuel for fire;
no one spares his brother.

¹⁹They hack on the right, but remain hungry;
they devour on the left, but are not filled.
Each devours the flesh of the neighbor;

continue

9:7–10:4 Judgment on Israel

Again the prophet moves back from his vision of the future to his indictment of the present. Though he sees the two Israelite kingdoms united under the rule of the Davidic dynasty some day, for the present the kingdom of Israel has to face judgment. The indictment has four particulars each concluding with the same refrain: "For all this, [God's] wrath is not turned back, / his hand is still outstretched!" (9:11, 16, 20; 10:4).

The first particular (9:7-11) denounces Israel for its arrogance. While the houses of the poor built with mud bricks and sycamore timber are collapsing, villas for the wealthy built from cedar and dressed stones are going up. This must end so God is stirring up Israel's neighbors whose military forays will destroy Israel and its corrupt economic and social system. The second particular (9:12-16) singles out Israel's elders and prophets who should have led the people with integrity. Their failure to meet their responsibilities will lead to devastation that will spare no one. Without competent leadership, society as a whole has become corrupt and will suffer under divine judgment.

The third particular (9:17-20) describes a society that is destroying itself through civil strife. Israel's social and economic system has degenerated to the extent that people see each other as enemies. They ought to have consid-

Assyrian warriors

ered each other brothers and sisters with whom they are to share the bounty that God has granted the land. Instead of this, they compete with each other for control of the nation's economic resources—a competition that has brought Israel to disaster. The final particular (10:1-4) indicts Israel for creating an economic system that steals from the defenseless. People of means are feeding themselves on the misery of the poor. They are guilty of economic cannibalism. Such a society dooms itself and that doom is what the prophet announced to Israel.

In Romans 9:27-28, Paul cites 10:22 to help explain the failure of the early Christian mission to the Jews. The apostle implies that God's promises never included all the people of Israel.

10:5-34 Assyria—God's instrument of judgment

The great achievement of the prophetic movement was to show the people of Israel that what happened to their two kingdoms fulfilled the purposes of their God. An alternative explanation of events held that the military defeat and political subjection of the Israelite kingdoms were due to the weakness of the Lord compared to the patron deities of the nations. Here the prophet explicitly identifies Assyria as God's instrument of judgment. The fall of the Israelite kingdoms, then, is not due to any failure on the Lord's part but is the result of Israel's failings.

The militarist and expansionist Assyrian Empire will be the means by which Israel and Judah will experience God's judgment on their social and economic systems. While the Assyrians have their own purposes for their conquest of the two Israelite kingdoms, Isaiah believes that these really serve God's purposes. The Assyrians wanted to take Egypt to secure its resources and to control the trade routes that connected Egypt to Mesopotamia. Between Assyria and Egypt lay the two Israelite kingdoms. These had to be taken in order for the Assyrian army to protect its lines of communication. The overwhelming power of Assyria's military and the confidence of its leaders sealed the fate of the two Israelite kingdoms (see map on p. 11).

²⁰Manasseh devours Ephraim, and Ephraim Manasseh,
together they turn on Judah.
For all this, his wrath is not turned back,
his hand is still outstretched!

CHAPTER 10

Perversion of Justice

¹Ah! Those who enact unjust statutes,
who write oppressive decrees,
²Depriving the needy of judgment,
robbing my people's poor of justice,
Making widows their plunder,
and orphans their prey!
³What will you do on the day of punishment,
when the storm comes from afar?
To whom will you flee for help?
Where will you leave your wealth,
⁴Lest it sink beneath the captive
or fall beneath the slain?
For all this, his wrath is not turned back,
his hand is still outstretched!

Judgment on Assyria

⁵Ah! Assyria, the rod of my wrath,
the staff I wield in anger.
⁶Against an impious nation I send him,
and against a people under my wrath I order him
To seize plunder, carry off loot,
and to trample them like the mud of the street.
⁷But this is not what he intends,
nor does he have this in mind;
Rather, it is in his heart to destroy,
to make an end of not a few nations.
⁸For he says, "Are not my commanders all kings?"
⁹"Is not Calno like Carchemish,
Or Hamath like Arpad,
or Samaria like Damascus?
¹⁰Just as my hand reached out to idolatrous kingdoms

continue

41

that had more images than Jerusalem and
Samaria—
[11]Just as I treated Samaria and her idols,
shall I not do to Jerusalem and her graven
images?"

[12]But when the LORD has brought to an end
all his work on Mount Zion and in Jerusalem,

I will punish the utterance
of the king of Assyria's proud heart,
and the boastfulness of his haughty eyes.
[13]For he says:
"By my own power I have done it,
and by my wisdom, for I am shrewd.
I have moved the boundaries of peoples,
their treasures I have pillaged,
and, like a mighty one, I have brought
down the enthroned.
[14]My hand has seized, like a nest,
the wealth of nations.
As one takes eggs left alone,
so I took in all the earth;
No one fluttered a wing,
or opened a mouth, or chirped!"
[15]Will the ax boast against the one who hews
with it?
Will the saw exalt itself above the one
who wields it?
As if a rod could sway the one who lifts it,
or a staff could lift the one who is not wood!
[16]Therefore the Lord, the LORD of hosts,
will send leanness among his fat ones,
And under his glory there will be a kindling
like the kindling of fire.
[17]The Light of Israel will become a fire,
the Holy One, a flame,
That burns and consumes its briers
and its thorns in a single day.
[18]And the glory of its forests and orchards
will be consumed, soul and body,
and it will be like a sick man who wastes
away.
[19]And the remnant of the trees in his forest
will be so few,

continue

The prophet saw the hand of God in the expansionist policies of the Assyrian Empire (10:5-11). The aberrant religious practices of the Israelite kingdoms served to provide religious support for their unjust social systems. The Israelite people came into existence by rejecting the religious systems of the nations in order to serve a God who took the side of slaves over their masters. The prophet decries the current religious practices of the Israelites who have subjected themselves to gods who support the greed of the people of means as they enrich themselves at the expense of the peasants. At God's direction, Assyria will bring an end to the religious folly of both Israel and Judah.

The Assyrians wished to establish a world empire, but the prophet insists that Israel's God has already done that. Though Assyria's expansionism is the means God has chosen to bring judgment on the Israelite kings, God will deal with Assyria for its arrogance. Assyria will face its own day of judgment (10:12). Before that happens, the Assyrian army will devastate the Israelite kingdoms. God's judgment will be like a forest fire that consumes almost everything in its path. There will be a few trees left, but these will serve simply to mark the movement of the divine judge through the land.

While the devastation of Israel's resources will be horrific, it will not be total. These few trees that survive the fire of God's judgment stand for the "remnant of Israel" that will survive (10:20). Judgment is never God's last word to Israel, and the remnant will be the means of Israel's survival. The importance of this motif for Isaiah is clear from the name he gave to his eldest son: "A remnant shall return" (7:3). Nonetheless, for the prophet the remnant motif involves a proclamation of judgment on unfaithful Judah: 10:19; 17:5-6; 30:17. Faith and conversion are necessary before the remnant can experience God's salvation. This will lead God to restore the remnant to the land from the nations where they have been exiled (11:11). Most of the occurrences of remnant language in Isaiah reflect political usage in which remnant describes what remained of a people who man-

that any child can record them.
²⁰On that day
The remnant of Israel,
  the survivors of the house of Jacob,
  will no more lean upon the one who
    struck them;
But they will lean upon the LORD,
  the Holy One of Israel, in truth.
²¹A remnant will return, the remnant of Jacob,
  to the mighty God.
²²Though your people, O Israel,
  were like the sand of the sea,
Only a remnant of them will return;
  their destruction is decreed,
  as overflowing justice demands.

²³For the Lord, the GOD of hosts, is about to carry out the destruction decreed in the midst of the whole land.

²⁴Therefore thus says the Lord, the GOD of hosts: My people, who dwell in Zion, do not fear the Assyrian, though he strikes you with a rod, and raises his staff against you as did the Egyptians. ²⁵For just a brief moment more, and my wrath shall be over, and my anger shall be set for their destruction. ²⁶Then the LORD of hosts will raise against them a scourge such as struck Midian

at the rock of Oreb; and he will raise his staff over the sea as he did in Egypt. ²⁷On that day,

His burden shall be taken from your shoulder,
  and his yoke shattered from your neck.

The March of an Enemy Army

He has come up from Rimmon,
  ²⁸he has reached Aiath, passed through
    Migron,
  at Michmash he has stored his supplies.
²⁹He has crossed the ravine,
  at Geba he has camped for the night.
Ramah trembles,
  Gibeah of Saul has fled.
³⁰Cry and shriek, Bath-Gallim!
  Hearken, Laishah! Answer her, Anathoth!
³¹Madmenah is in flight,
  the inhabitants of Gebim seek refuge.
³²Even today he will halt at Nob,
  he will shake his fist at the mount of
    daughter Zion,
  the hill of Jerusalem!
³³Now the Lord, the LORD of hosts,
  is about to lop off the boughs with
    terrible violence;

continue

aged to survive a military campaign that aimed at their total destruction.

There are several texts from the book of Isaiah in which the remnant idea is defined as a miraculously preserved minority (4:3; 10:20; and 38:5). This idea meshes with a principal Isaianic theme: Jerusalem is threatened but ultimately delivered. In Isaiah the remnant motif is part of the prophet's call for repentance and faith. Still, Isaiah says practically nothing about the identity of this remnant. Zephaniah, a Judahite prophet who lived about two hundred years after Isaiah, is not so reticent and identifies the remnant with the poor (Zeph 2:3; 3:12-13). They will survive the judgment and be the nucleus of a new people of God.

 Isaiah 10:26 refers to the **miraculous victory** that Gideon, leading a small group of warriors, achieved over the entire Midianite army in Judges 7. Here Isaiah chooses an especially apt example of God's power to protect and defend God's people, for the size of Gideon's force was arranged by divine decree so that Israel could not say "[m]y own power saved me" but would recognize and acknowledge that the victory came through God's might alone (Judg 7:2).

The poem in verses 28-34 describes with geographical detail the Assyrian advance on Jeru-

The tall of stature shall be felled,
and the lofty ones shall be brought low;
³⁴He shall hack down the forest thickets with
an ax,
and Lebanon in its splendor shall fall.

CHAPTER 11

The Ideal Davidic King

¹But a shoot shall sprout from the stump of
Jesse,
and from his roots a bud shall blossom.
²The spirit of the LORD shall rest upon him:
a spirit of wisdom and of understanding,
A spirit of counsel and of strength,
a spirit of knowledge and of fear of the
LORD,
³and his delight shall be the fear of the
LORD.
Not by appearance shall he judge,
nor by hearsay shall he decide,
⁴But he shall judge the poor with justice,
and decide fairly for the land's afflicted.
He shall strike the ruthless with the rod of
his mouth,
and with the breath of his lips he shall
slay the wicked.
⁵Justice shall be the band around his waist,
and faithfulness a belt upon his hips.
⁶Then the wolf shall be a guest of the lamb,
and the leopard shall lie down with the
young goat;
The calf and the young lion shall browse
together,
with a little child to guide them.
⁷The cow and the bear shall graze,
together their young shall lie down;
the lion shall eat hay like the ox.
⁸The baby shall play by the viper's den,
and the child lay his hand on the adder's
lair.
⁹They shall not harm or destroy on all my
holy mountain;

continue

salem from the north. It appears that nothing can stand in the way of the Assyrian invader. Still, God, who is called here "the LORD of hosts" ("host" being a traditional term for "army") prevents the Assyrians from taking Zion. Instead, the Assyrians themselves suffer a great defeat.

11:1-9 The shoot from Jesse

The prophet shifts away from political and military realities back into an idealistic vision of the future. As in 9:2-7, Isaiah gives a central place in that future to an ideal king who will be everything that Judah's actual kings were not.

God's promise regarding Judah's future will find its fulfillment through a descendant of Jesse, the father of David. The "shoot . . . from the stump of Jesse" is an engaging poetic metaphor for an ideal king who will be equipped for his rule by God's spirit. This will insure his success. This savior-king will be known for his judicial wisdom, his ability to translate his decisions into action, his attitude toward the poor, his readiness to deal harshly with evildoers, his devotion to God, and his righteousness (11:2-5). The rule of this coming king will please both God and God's people.

The coming of this ideal king will be marked by the taming of wild animals (11:6-8). At present people have to fear for the safety of their domestic animals and their children. The prophet envisions a future when this danger will be removed; however, he is clear that this change will take place only when all people act righteously in accord with the guidance provided by the savior-king (11:9b). The absence of this "knowledge . . . of the LORD" is the reason for alienation from God and the consequent divine judgment (1:3; 5:13; 6:10). The knowledge the prophet speaks of is not information about God but a commitment to God and traditional Israelite moral values.

At the end of his infancy narrative, Matthew states that Joseph settled his family in Nazareth to fulfill the prophetic word that "He shall be called a Nazorean" (Matt 2:23). There is no such text in the Hebrew Bible, though there is a similarity in sound between the Aramaic word for

Nazareth and the Hebrew word that the NABRE translates as "shoot" in verse 1. Of course, Christian believers have claimed that this prophetic vision of a second David has been fulfilled in Jesus. The expectations of the prophet, however, were not fulfilled in a literal sense but were reinterpreted by people of faith. Religious Jews continue to look for the coming of the king that the prophet describes. Both Jews and Christians together wait for the final revelation of God's power and glory in a completely definitive way.

The redemption that the prophet describes is not directed at the salvation of individual people. The coming of this ideal king will involve the renewal of all creation. Because the world is God's creation, it will not devolve into nothingness, but will be transformed and renewed in the final consummation which both Jew and Christian still await.

11:10-16 Israel and Judah united

Speaking of the rule of the ideal king leads the prophet to speak of the kingdom over which that king will rule. For most of their history, the two Israelite kingdoms were antagonistic to one another with Israel, the more powerful of the two usually taking the upper hand. What the prophet envisions are the two kingdoms united under the rule of a single sovereign from the "root of Jesse," i.e., the Davidic dynasty. Before that vision can find fulfillment, God will first have to gather the remnant of the two kingdoms that have been dispersed through exile. Once this remnant has been assembled, there will be no evidence of the rivalry that had marked the relations between Israel (Ephraim) and Judah. The new united people will enjoy sovereignty over neighboring national states. The prophet compares this future act of deliverance to the exodus from Egypt that transformed the Hebrew slaves into the people of God.

In Romans 15:8-12, Paul cites several texts including verse 10 to emphasize that, while Jesus' being a Jew proves God's fidelity to the promises made to the patriarchs, the salvation promised was for the Gentiles as well.

for the earth shall be filled with
knowledge of the LORD,
as water covers the sea.

Restoration

¹⁰On that day,
The root of Jesse,
set up as a signal for the peoples—
Him the nations will seek out;
his dwelling shall be glorious.
¹¹On that day,
The Lord shall again take it in hand
to reclaim the remnant of his people
that is left from Assyria and Egypt,
Pathros, Ethiopia, and Elam,
Shinar, Hamath, and the isles of the sea.
¹²He shall raise a signal to the nations
and gather the outcasts of Israel;
The dispersed of Judah he shall assemble
from the four corners of the earth.
¹³The envy of Ephraim shall pass away,
and those hostile to Judah shall be cut off;
Ephraim shall not envy Judah,
and Judah shall not be hostile to
Ephraim;
¹⁴But they shall swoop down on the foothills
of the Philistines to the west,
together they shall plunder the people of
the east;
Edom and Moab shall be their possessions,
and the Ammonites their subjects.
¹⁵The LORD shall dry up the tongue of the
Sea of Egypt,
and wave his hand over the Euphrates
with his fierce wind,
And divide it into seven streamlets,
so that it can be crossed in sandals.
¹⁶There shall be a highway for the remnant of
his people
that is left from Assyria,
As there was for Israel
when it came up from the land of Egypt.

EXPLORING LESSON TWO

1. Compare the "Song of the Vineyard" in Isaiah (5:1-7) with Jesus' parable of the vineyard (Matt 21:33-41). What similarities strike you? What differences stand out to you? (See also Jer 2:21; Ezek 19:10-12; Hos 10:1; Luke 13:6-9.)

_____

_____

_____

_____

_____

2. Describe a time when you have felt the majestic presence of God, or some other experience of God's presence, as Isaiah did in 6:1-7.

_____

_____

_____

_____

3. What are the seraphim that are part of Isaiah's vision of God in the temple (6:2)? (See Num 21:4-9.)

_____

_____

_____

_____

4. a) What sign does Isaiah say God is giving Ahaz to assure him that Judah will survive an attack by Samaria and Aram (7:10-16)?

_____

_____

_____

b) How is this sign given special importance in the Gospel of Matthew (Matt 1:18-23)?

_____

_____

_____

_____

5. a) Instead of military foes, who is the real "rock for stumbling" and "trap" and "snare" that the people of Judah should be fearing (8:12-15)?

_____

_____

_____

_____

   b) How does Paul make use of Isaiah 8:14 in Romans 9:30-33?

_____

_____

_____

_____

6. What is the promised "great light" that will be given to "those who lived in a land of gloom" (9:1-6)? (See Matt 4:12-17.)

_____

_____

_____

_____

_____

7. What four reasons does Isaiah give for God's pending judgment of the northern kingdom of Israel (9:7-11, 12-16, 17-20; 10:1-4)?

_____

_____

_____

_____

_____

8. What life lessons have you learned after enduring difficult times (10:20)?

_____

_____

_____

_____

_____

9. Who is Jesse, and why is he said to be a "stump" (11:1)? (See 1 Sam 16:1-13.)

_____

_____

_____

_____

_____

10. Of the many spiritual gifts that are to be bestowed on the future king (11:2), which one do you think is the most important for leaders in our faith communities today? Which of these gifts do you pray for most fervently in your own life?

_____

_____

_____

_____

_____

CLOSING PRAYER

Prayer

The people who walked in darkness
have seen a great light;
Upon those who lived in a land of gloom
a light has shone. (Isa 9:1)

Father, we believe that your promise of a great light shining in the darkness has been fulfilled in the birth of your Son. May our gratitude for this gift be unceasing, and may our joy in his presence be eternal. In thanksgiving for the light that has forever dispelled the darkness of sin, sadness, and death, we vow to be bearers of light in our families, workplaces, and communities, especially by . . .

LESSON THREE

Isaiah 12–19

Begin your personal study and group discussion with a simple and sincere prayer such as:

Prayer

Heavenly Father, as we read the words of your prophet Isaiah, help us respond to his call to repentance and a new way of life. May our study inspire us to imitate you, the pillar of justice and the fountain of all mercy.

Read the Bible text of Isaiah 12–19 found in the outside columns of pages 50–62, highlighting what stands out to you.

Read the accompanying commentary to add to your understanding.

Respond to the questions on pages 63–65, Exploring Lesson Three.

The Closing Prayer on page 66 is for your personal use and may be used at the end of group discussion.

CHAPTER 12

Song of Thanksgiving

¹On that day, you will say:
I give you thanks, O LORD;
> though you have been angry with me,
> your anger has abated, and you have
> consoled me.

²God indeed is my salvation;
> I am confident and unafraid.
For the LORD is my strength and my might,
> and he has been my salvation.

³With joy you will draw water
> from the fountains of salvation,

⁴And you will say on that day:
> give thanks to the LORD, acclaim his
> name;
Among the nations make known his deeds,
> proclaim how exalted is his name.

⁵Sing praise to the LORD for he has done
> glorious things;
let this be known throughout all the
> earth.

⁶Shout with exultation, City of Zion,
> for great in your midst
> is the Holy One of Israel!

continue

sense only if there is to be a future for Judah. This hymn of salvation expresses the prophet's assurance that divine judgment will not be the end of Judah but the beginning of a new act of salvation.

 Isaiah's use of **water as a symbol of salvation** (12:3) is similar to the use of this imagery in several other Old Testament prophets, including Ezekiel (47:1), Hosea (6:3), Joel (4:18), and Zechariah (14:8). In Jeremiah, God is twice referred to as the "source of living waters" (2:13; 17:13), a role that Jesus himself will assume in the Gospel of John (4:14; 7:38).

12:1-6 A hymn of salvation

This is a short hymn of thanksgiving for Jerusalem's deliverance. While Isaiah was certain that Jerusalem was going to experience divine judgment for the failure of its leaders to maintain a just society, he was equally convinced that judgment on Jerusalem was not final. One call to praise and thanksgiving follows another as the prophet exclaims his confidence in Zion's future. One can look beyond judgment to a glorious future for Zion because the Holy One of Israel remains in the midst of the city. While the mission of the prophet was to confront Judah with the consequences of its failure to maintain a just society, there was another aspect to that mission that cannot be ignored. The prophet's mission makes

JERUSALEM AND THE NATIONS

Isaiah 13:1–27:13

The prophets addressed their words to a real people, who lived at a real time and in a real place, and who had to deal with real problems. Among the most serious of these problems were the political and military pressures brought to bear upon the Israelite kingdoms by neighboring national states and imperial powers. Economic and political realities usually meant that ancient Israel regarded its neighbors as potential threats to its existence. In speaking about Jerusalem's future, Isaiah could not avoid speaking about the nations. In this second section of the book, the dominant attitude toward the nations is negative since these oracles reflect the experience of Israel and Judah with the nations. For most of their history, the two Israelite kingdoms had to contend with the other national states in the eastern Mediterranean region for control of the region's commercial and agricultural resources. The kingdom of Israel's principal rivals were Aram and Moab, while Judah's were the Philistine city-states and Edom. The two Israelite kingdoms contended with each other as well, with Israel having the most success. But it was the rise of the neo-Assyrian and neo-Babylonian empires with their aggressive and expansionist policies that led to the end of first Israel and then Judah as national states.

Oracles against the nations are a prominent feature in several prophetic books, e.g., Amos 1:2–2:3; Jeremiah 46:1–51:64; and Ezekiel 25–32. Indeed, an oracle against Assyria comprises the whole of the book of Nahum. Since the people of the two Israelite kingdoms experienced other nations as threats to their existence, it is not surprising that they called upon their God to defend them from such threats. The oracles against the nations are an expression of ancient Israel's belief that God would never permit these nations to destroy Israel completely. While God has chosen to use these nations to bring judgment upon the Israelite kingdoms for their failure to maintain a just society, God will move against these nations for their failures as well. God's judgment of the nations will mean salvation for Israel.

Some modern readers find these oracles difficult to read. First, the nations against whom the prophet announces God's judgment are simply geographical names devoid of any emotional content. But the prophet's first audience reacted to names like Assyria, Edom, Philistia, and Babylon the same way that the Irish react to England, the Tibetans to China, the Bosnians to Serbia, and the Koreans to Japan. Second, some of the prophet's modern readers are shocked by the harshness of the prophet's words. While the severity of the judgments pronounced by the prophet reflects rhetorical pat-

---

CHAPTER 13

Babylon.

¹An oracle concerning Babylon; a vision of Isaiah, son of Amoz.

²Upon the bare mountains set up a signal;
   cry out to them,
Beckon for them to enter
   the gates of the nobles.
³I have commanded my consecrated ones,
   I have summoned my warriors,
   eager and bold to carry out my anger.
⁴Listen! the rumble on the mountains:
   that of an immense throng!
Listen! the noise of kingdoms, nations
   assembled!
The LORD of hosts is mustering
   an army for battle.
⁵They come from a far-off country,
   and from the end of the heavens,
The LORD and the instruments of his wrath,
   to destroy all the land.

continue

---

terns of his culture, it also displays an anger that is genuine. There may be a holdover of this attitude toward the nations when Jesus refers to the Syrophoenician woman and her daughter as "dogs" (Mark 7:27-28). Certainly, the book of Revelation is as harsh toward Rome as any of the Old Testament's oracles against the nations.

Like the first section of the book, this one also begins with an oracle of judgment against arrogance and injustice, though here the oracle is addressed to Babylon rather than Judah. Again, as was the case with the previous section, this second section of the book ends on a positive note. The prophet announces salvation for Judah.

13:1–14:23 Against Babylon

First place among the nations under divine judgment is given to Babylon. The events that led to the production of Isaiah as we have it and, indeed, a good part of the Old Testament

⁶Howl, for the day of the LORD is near;
    as destruction from the Almighty it comes.
⁷Therefore all hands fall helpless,
    every human heart melts,
⁸and they are terrified,
Pangs and sorrows take hold of them,
    like a woman in labor they writhe;
They look aghast at each other,
    their faces aflame.
⁹Indeed, the day of the LORD comes,
    cruel, with wrath and burning anger;
To lay waste the land
    and destroy the sinners within it!
¹⁰The stars of the heavens and their
        constellations
    will send forth no light;
The sun will be dark at its rising,
    and the moon will not give its light.
¹¹Thus I will punish the world for its evil
    and the wicked for their guilt.
I will put an end to the pride of the arrogant,
    the insolence of tyrants I will humble.
¹²I will make mortals more rare than pure gold,
    human beings, than the gold of Ophir.
¹³For this I will make the heavens tremble
    and the earth shall be shaken from its place,

continue

in its present form were those surrounding the Babylonian conquest of Jerusalem in 587 B.C. and the fall of Babylon less than fifty years later. The fall of this mighty empire and the subsequent restoration of Jerusalem and its temple gave Judah hope for the future. It is fitting, then, that the first of the oracles against the nations has Babylon as its subject. The ascription of this oracle to the eighth-century prophet is appropriate because of his insistence that divine judgment upon Judah, though well deserved, was not God's final word to Jerusalem. While the nations are God's instruments of judgment, they will have to answer for their own excesses, arrogance, and folly.

Babylon was among the largest cities of the ancient world. Its ruins are in the vicinity of modern Baghdad, and excavation of the ancient site began in the early twentieth century. The glazed bricks from the top of Babylon's Ishtar Gate attracted archaeologists to the site. Archaeologists have also excavated portions of an inner and outer city wall, three palaces, and four temples, as well as domestic architecture. Scholarly interest centered on the city's ziggurat (a stepped tower) because of its association with the tower of Babel (Gen 11:1-9), but little beyond the base of the ziggurat has survived.

This poem opens with Babylon's sentinels sounding the alarm as an army of conquest is approaching the city. The marching feet of its immense horde moving toward the city make sounds like the rumble of thunder on a distant mountain as the storm gathers strength and begins its approach. Of course, it is Judah's God who has gathered

Illustration of Ishtar Gate (center) and ziggurat in the ancient city of Babylon

this mighty force against Babylon, whose military forces desert as the army assembled by God approaches. The portents in the heavens make it obvious that this is no ordinary military adventure, but one directed by God. The devastation will be complete and Babylon will experience the horrors of war. The Medes, who are God's chosen instruments of judgment, will turn Babylon into a wasteland.

The prophet uses a type of hyperbole that often appears in biblical texts with a high emotional content. The poem is trying to revive the spirit of the Judahite community that was devastated by the fall of Jerusalem, the destruction of its temple, and the exile of a sizeable portion of its population. Many of the exiles accommodated themselves to the new realities. The prophet insists that Babylon has no future and implies that its fall is a harbinger of a new future for Judah. The fall of Babylon makes Judah's restoration possible. The prophet elaborates on this reversal of fortunes as he taunts Babylon. He asserts that the exile will be reversed: instead of the people of Israel being led off to Babylon as slaves, the Babylonians will be led to the land of Israel to serve the community restored to its native land. Of course, here the prophet is becoming carried away by his own rhetoric.

 Hyperbole (exaggeration) is a rhetorical device used for emphasis in both the Old and New Testaments. God's utter disdain for temple ritual and sacrifice in Amos 5:21 is one example; Jesus' counsel for self-mutilation in Matthew 5:29-30 is another. In both texts, hyperbole is used to underscore the seriousness of the lesson being taught (the worthlessness of mindless worship in the first instance, and the absolute necessity of avoiding sin in the second).

The oracle in 14:4b-21 begins by proclaiming the fall of the tyrant responsible for the oppression of many nations, all of whom delight

At the wrath of the LORD of hosts
    on the day of his burning anger.
¹⁴Like a hunted gazelle,
    or a flock that no one gathers,
They shall turn each to their own people
    and flee each to their own land.
¹⁵Everyone who is taken shall be run through;
    and everyone who is caught shall fall by
        the sword.
¹⁶Their infants shall be dashed to pieces in
        their sight;
    their houses shall be plundered
    and their wives ravished.
¹⁷I am stirring up against them the Medes,
    who think nothing of silver
    and take no delight in gold.
¹⁸With their bows they shall shatter the
        young men,
And the fruit of the womb they shall not
        spare,
    nor shall their eye take pity on children.
¹⁹And Babylon, the jewel of kingdoms,
    the glory and pride of the Chaldeans,
Shall become like Sodom and Gomorrah,
    overthrown by God.
²⁰It shall never be inhabited,
    nor dwelt in, from age to age;
Arabians shall not pitch their tents there,
    nor shepherds rest their flocks there.
²¹But desert demons shall rest there
    and owls shall fill the houses;
There ostriches shall dwell,
    and satyrs shall dance.
²²Wild dogs shall dwell in its castles,
    and jackals in its luxurious palaces.
Its time is near at hand
    and its days shall not be prolonged.

CHAPTER 14

Restoration of Israel

¹But the LORD will take pity on Jacob and again choose Israel, and will settle them on their own land; foreigners will join them and attach

continue

themselves to the house of Jacob. ²The nations will take them and bring them to their place, and the house of Israel will possess them as male and female slaves on the Lord's land; they will take captive their captors and rule over their oppressors.

Downfall of the King of Babylon

³On the day when the LORD gives you rest from your sorrow and turmoil, from the hard service with which you served, ⁴you will take up this taunt-song against the king of Babylon:

How the oppressor has come to an end!
  how the turmoil has ended!
⁵The LORD has broken the rod of the wicked,
  the staff of the tyrants
⁶That struck the peoples in wrath
  with relentless blows;
That ruled the nations in anger,
  with boundless persecution.
⁷The whole earth rests peacefully,
  song breaks forth;
⁸The very cypresses rejoice over you,
  the cedars of Lebanon:
"Now that you are laid to rest,
  no one comes to cut us down."
⁹Below, Sheol is all astir
  preparing for your coming;
Awakening the shades to greet you,
  all the leaders of the earth;
Making all the kings of the nations
  rise from their thrones.
¹⁰All of them speak out
  and say to you,
"You too have become weak like us,
  you are just like us!
¹¹Down to Sheol your pomp is brought,
  the sound of your harps.
Maggots are the couch beneath you,
  worms your blanket."
¹²How you have fallen from the heavens,
  O Morning Star, son of the dawn!
How you have been cut down to the earth,
  you who conquered nations!

continue

in the tyrant's fall. Peace has come again to the world. The trees of Lebanon's lush forests are personified to represent the nations who are relieved to know there will be no one to cut them down again.

Tyrants of the distant past welcome the king of Babylon to their realm in the nether world. He is now one of them, exchanging the accouterments of a regal life style for the worms that devour the corpses of the dead. Babylon's king did not even have the benefit of a decent burial. His corpse is simply trampled underfoot. This terrible fate is due him because of his failures as a king. His sons will also be killed to insure that his name will be forgotten. The oracle against Babylon concludes with a prose statement (14:22-23) in which God affirms the decision to destroy Babylon totally. The book of Revelation adopts Babylon as its code name for Rome, which it perceived as a threat to the existence of the early Christian community.

The New Testament uses the imagery of 13:10 in speaking about the end of the age (Matt 24:29; Mark 13:24-25; Luke 21:25; Rev 6:12-13; 8:12). In 14:12 the prophet calls the king of Babylon the "Morning Star," which Jerome rendered into Latin as "Lucifer." Patristic and medieval interpreters, influenced by Jerome and connecting Isaiah 14:12 with Luke 10:18, read this passage as a description of the fall of rebellious angels. Of course, this interpretation is an example of creative imagination. Still, Lucifer has passed into popular language as a name for the leader of the fallen angels.

The terrible upheaval predicted by Isaiah's prophecy of the "**day of the LORD**" (13:9-10) resembles similar descriptions found in other prophets, especially in reference to the total darkness that will accompany it. Zephaniah predicts that "the great day of the LORD" will be a "day of darkness and gloom" (1:14-15), while Jeremiah proclaims that before the "blazing anger" of God, the lights of the heavens will go out, and the earth shall mourn in darkness (4:23-28).

¹³In your heart you said:
"I will scale the heavens;
Above the stars of God
  I will set up my throne;
I will take my seat on the Mount of Assembly,
  on the heights of Zaphon.
¹⁴I will ascend above the tops of the clouds;
  I will be like the Most High!"
¹⁵No! Down to Sheol you will be brought
  to the depths of the pit!
¹⁶When they see you they will stare,
  pondering over you:
"Is this the man who made the earth tremble,
  who shook kingdoms?
¹⁷Who made the world a wilderness,
  razed its cities,
  and gave captives no release?"
¹⁸All the kings of the nations lie in glory,
  each in his own tomb;
¹⁹But you are cast forth without burial,
  like loathsome carrion,
Covered with the slain, with those struck by
  the sword,
  a trampled corpse,
Going down to the very stones of the pit.
²⁰You will never be together with them in
  the grave,
For you have ruined your land,
  you have slain your people!
Let him never be named,
  that offshoot of evil!

²¹Make ready to slaughter his sons
  for the guilt of their fathers;
Lest they rise and possess the earth,
  and fill the breadth of the world with
  cities.

²²I will rise up against them, says the LORD of hosts, and cut off from Babylon name and remnant, progeny and offspring, says the LORD. ²³I will make it a haunt of hoot owls and a marshland; I will sweep it with the broom of destruction, oracle of the LORD of hosts.

God's Plan for Assyria

²⁴The LORD of hosts has sworn:
As I have resolved,
  so shall it be;
As I have planned,
  so shall it stand:
²⁵To break the Assyrian in my land
  and trample him on my mountains;
Then his yoke shall be removed from them,
  and his burden from their shoulder.
²⁶This is the plan proposed for the whole
  earth,
  and this the hand outstretched over all
  the nations.
²⁷The LORD of hosts has planned;
  who can thwart him?
His hand is stretched out;
  who can turn it back?

continue

14:24-27 Against Assyria

The aggressively expansionist neo-Assyrian empire made a series of incursions into the territory of the two Israelite kingdoms during the last third of the eighth century B.C. This oracle implies that God would destroy the Assyrian Empire during one of those incursions. While the Assyrian army was besieging Jerusalem in 701 B.C., civil unrest back in Assyria required the return of the army. Perhaps the oracle refers to the lifting of that siege (Isa 37:36-37; 2 Kgs 19:35-37). In any case, the Assyrian Empire fell in 612

B.C. to the Babylonians (see map on p. 12). Certainly the prophet wanted to insure that the people of Judah would see the working out of a divine purpose in the collapse of that empire. Again, the fall of a great empire was a sign of God's power and determination to rehabilitate Judah and Jerusalem.

14:28-32 Against Philistia

The prophet had already asserted that God used the Philistines to punish Israel for its infidelity (9:11). Now he warns the Philistines

Philistia

²⁸In the year that King Ahaz died, there came this oracle:

²⁹Do not rejoice, Philistia, not one of you,
  that the rod which struck you is broken;
For out of the serpent's root shall come an
  adder,
  its offspring shall be a flying saraph.
³⁰In my pastures the poor shall graze,
  and the needy lie down in safety;
But I will kill your root with famine
  that shall slay even your remnant.
³¹Howl, O gate; cry out, O city!
  Philistia, all of you melts away!
For there comes a smoke from the north,
  without a straggler in its ranks.
³²What will one answer the messengers of
  the nations?
"The LORD has established Zion,
  and in her the afflicted of his people find
  refuge."

CHAPTER 15

Moab

¹Oracle on Moab:
Laid waste in a night,
  Ar of Moab is destroyed;
Laid waste in a night,
  Kir of Moab is destroyed.
²Daughter Dibon has gone up
  to the high places to weep;
Over Nebo and over Medeba
  Moab is wailing.
Every head is shaved,
  every beard sheared off.
³In the streets they wear sackcloth,
  and on the rooftops;
In the squares
  everyone wails, streaming with tears.
⁴Heshbon and Elealeh cry out,
  they are heard as far as Jahaz.
At this the loins of Moab tremble,

continue

that they, in turn, will face their day of judgment. Like all the peoples who lived along the eastern Mediterranean coast, the Philistines were subjugated by Assyria. Though Assyria has fallen, the Philistines should not be too quick to celebrate. Another serpent whose venom is even stronger than that of the Assyrians will strike them. Of course, Babylon, whom the prophet characterizes as a "flying saraph," is that foe from the north who will bring an end to the Philistine cities that harassed Judah in its weakness. Philistia's trouble is Jerusalem's salvation.

15:1–16:14 Against Moab

Moab too had to deal with the Assyrian incursions into its territory. Unlike the two Israelite kingdoms, Moab was much more compliant. It even assisted the Assyrians in dealing with Arab tribes who resisted Assyrian domination. This collaboration with Assyria may have led the prophet to include Moab among the nations that were to experience divine judgment. The oracle likely reflects the result of a later Babylonian campaign in the region that ended the existence of Moab as a political entity. It describes the total devastation that affected every major Moabite city as well as the surrounding countryside. The humiliations that come with occupation led the people to ritual mourning whose purpose was to induce the gods to have pity on them, but it had no effect. Moab's ruination continued and its people fled before the invader, but many did not escape.

Some of Moab's refugees will make their way to Zion, where they will seek to escape the Babylonian forces invading their homeland. Though these refugees will find protection, nothing can be done to stop the total devastation of their homeland. What was once a formidable power in the region will barely survive the Babylonian invasion. The Moabites will lament and pray but without effect. Nothing can stop what will happen to their country. The prophet assures his readers that Moab will indeed experience God's judgment. There will only be a small and weak remnant left of what was once a significant regional power. Of

his soul quivers within him;
⁵My heart cries out for Moab,
    his fugitives reach Zoar,
    Eglath-shelishiyah:
The ascent of Luhith
    they ascend weeping;
On the way to Horonaim
    they utter rending cries;
⁶The waters of Nimrim
    have become a waste,
The grass is withered,
    new growth is gone,
    nothing is green.
⁷So now whatever they have acquired or
    stored away
    they carry across the Wadi of the Poplars.
⁸The cry has gone round
    the territory of Moab;
As far as Eglaim his wailing,
    even at Beer-elim his wailing.
⁹The waters of Dimon are filled with blood,
    but I will bring still more upon Dimon:
Lions for those who are fleeing from Moab
    and for those who remain in the land!

CHAPTER 16

¹Send them forth, hugging the earth like reptiles,
    from Sela across the desert,
    to the mount of daughter Zion.
²Like flushed birds,
    like scattered nestlings,
Are the daughters of Moab
    at the fords of the Arnon.
³Offer counsel, take their part;
    at high noon make your shade like the
        night;
Hide the outcasts,
    do not betray the fugitives.
⁴Let the outcasts of Moab live with you,
    be their shelter from the destroyer.
When there is an end to the oppressor,
    when destruction has ceased,
    and the marauders have vanished from
        the land,

⁵A throne shall be set up in mercy,
    and on it shall sit in fidelity,
    in David's tent,
A judge upholding right,
    prompt to do justice.
⁶We have heard of the pride of Moab,
    how very proud he is,
Of his haughtiness, pride, and arrogance
    that his empty words do not match.
⁷Therefore let Moab wail,
    let everyone wail for Moab;
For the raisin cakes of Kir-hareseth
    let them sigh, stricken with grief.
⁸The terraced slopes of Heshbon languish,
    the vines of Sibmah,
Whose clusters once overpowered
    the lords of nations,
Reaching as far as Jazer
    winding through the wilderness,
Whose branches spread forth,
    crossing over the sea.
⁹Therefore I weep with Jazer
    for the vines of Sibmah;
I drench you with my tears,
    Heshbon and Elealeh;
For on your summer fruits and harvests
    the battle cry has fallen.
¹⁰From the orchards are taken away
    joy and gladness,
In the vineyards there is no singing,
    no shout of joy;
In the wine presses no one treads grapes,
    the vintage shout is stilled.
¹¹Therefore for Moab
    my heart moans like a lyre,
    my inmost being for Kir-hareseth.
¹²When Moab wears himself out on the high
        places,
    and enters his sanctuary to pray,
    it shall avail him nothing.

¹³That is the word the LORD spoke against Moab in times past. ¹⁴But now the LORD speaks: In three years, like the years of a hired laborer, the

continue

glory of Moab shall be empty despite all its great multitude; and the remnant shall be very small and weak.

CHAPTER 17

Damascus

¹Oracle on Damascus:
See, Damascus shall cease to be a city
and become a pile of ruins;
²Her cities shall be forever abandoned,
for flocks to lie in undisturbed.
³The fortress shall vanish from Ephraim
and dominion from Damascus;
The remnant of Aram shall become like the glory
of the Israelites—
oracle of the LORD of hosts.
⁴On that day
The glory of Jacob shall fade,
and his full body shall grow thin.
⁵Like the reaper's mere armful of stalks,
when he gathers the standing grain;
Or as when one gleans the ears
in the Valley of Rephaim.
⁶Only gleanings shall be left in it,
as when an olive tree has been beaten—
Two or three olives at the very top,
four or five on its most fruitful branches—
oracle of the LORD, the God of Israel.
⁷On that day people shall turn to their maker,
their eyes shall look to the Holy One of Israel.
⁸They shall not turn to the altars, the work of their hands,
nor shall they look to what their fingers have made:
the asherahs or the incense stands.
⁹On that day his strong cities shall be
like those abandoned by the Hivites and Amorites
When faced with the Israelites;
and there shall be desolation.

continue

course, the remnant of Judah will be the instrument that God will use to restore Jerusalem.

17:1-6 Against Damascus

Damascus was the capital of Aram (Syria), a one-time rival of the kingdom of Israel and then its ally against the encroachments of the Assyrians. When Ahaz, the king of Judah, refused to join their anti-Assyrian coalition, Aram and Israel were preparing to invade Judah to depose Ahaz and replace him with a more cooperative monarch. Isaiah was certain that these plans would fail (7:1–8:4). The prophet knew the ferocity of the Assyrian military machine. He was sure that the Assyrians would give those arrayed against them no quarter. Hardly anything will be left of Aram and Israel once the Assyrians move against them. The inevitable Assyrian response will cause terrible devastation to cities and villages throughout both Aram and Israel. The destructive forces of the Assyrian army would leave as little behind as do harvesters in a wheat field or on an olive tree.

17:7-11 Against the worship of other gods

The metaphor comparing the Assyrian army to harvesters led the prophet to inveigh against the worship of other gods, which was so offensive to someone who believed in the holiness of Judah's God and in the exclusive claims that God had on Judah. What the people of Judah expected from their God was fertility for the land and protection from enemies. They sought these not only from the Lord, their patron deity, but from other gods as well. Here the prophet mentions the trappings of non-Yahwistic worship as a cause of shame for the people of Judah. The "foreign" god of verse 10 is likely Tammuz, a god connected with grain production. The prophet asserts that those who sought to secure a good harvest through rituals associated with Tammuz (see also Ezek 8:14-15) will find that all their activity was in vain and they will enjoy no harvest at all.

The **"asherahs"** referred to in 17:8 were cultic objects sacred to the Canaanite goddess Asherah, who was the consort of Baal, a storm god. The objects, likely made of wood, were fashioned in the form of a stake or pole. It is assumed that asherahs may have been carved with symbols sacred to the goddess or may have been fashioned in her image. Destruction of asherahs was a hallmark of the religious reforms of King Josiah (see 2 Kgs 23:4-15).

An asherah

The judgment against Israel and Aram will lead Judah to recognize the claims that its national God makes upon it. Judah will see the folly of serving other gods. They will reject all forms of non-Yahwistic religion. Those people who do not will lose their claim to the land just as their ancestors dispossessed earlier inhabitants of the land.

> ¹⁰Truly, you have forgotten the God who
> saves you,
> the Rock, your refuge, you have not
> remembered.
> Therefore, though you plant plants for the
> Pleasant One,
> and set out cuttings for a foreign one,
> ¹¹Though you make them grow the day you
> plant them
> and make them blossom the morning you
> set them out,
> The harvest shall disappear on a day of
> sickness
> and incurable pain.
> ¹²Ah! the roaring of many peoples—
> a roar like the roar of the seas!
> The thundering of nations—
> thunder like the thundering of mighty
> waters!
> ¹³But God shall rebuke them,
> and they shall flee far away,
> Driven like chaff on the mountains before a
> wind,
> like tumbleweed before a storm.
> ¹⁴At evening, there is terror,
> but before morning, they are gone!
> Such is the portion of those who despoil us,
> the lot of those who plunder us.
>
> *continue*

17:12-14 Against the nations

To summarize the oracles against the two great Mesopotamian empires and three local powers, the prophet composed a short poem on the power of God. He used an old metaphor from the ancient Near Eastern religious tradition: the power of God as manifested in the control of the unruly and potentially chaotic sea. The peoples of the ancient Near East believed the greatest manifestation of divine power was keeping the power of the sea in check. The story of creation begins with the "spirit of God" moving over the sea and bringing order and life to what was void and without form (Gen 1:2).

The prophet asserts that God can bring order out of the chaos unleashed by the greed and ferocity of the nations. Though these nations look strong and appear ready to overwhelm Judah, they will not succeed. Their threats will disappear as quickly and suddenly as they appeared. The prophet believes that

CHAPTER 18

Ethiopia

¹Ah! Land of buzzing insects,
    beyond the rivers of Ethiopia,
²Sending ambassadors by sea,
    in papyrus boats on the waters!
Go, swift messengers,
    to a nation tall and bronzed,
To a people dreaded near and far,
    a nation strong and conquering,
    whose land is washed by rivers.
³All you who inhabit the world,
    who dwell on earth,
When the signal is raised on the mountain,
    look!
When the trumpet blows, listen!
⁴For thus says the LORD to me:
    I will be quiet, looking on from where I
      dwell,
Like the shimmering heat in sunshine,
    like a cloud of dew at harvest time.
⁵Before the vintage, when the flowering has
    ended,
    and the blooms are succeeded by ripening
      grapes,
Then comes the cutting of branches with
    pruning hooks,
    and the discarding of the lopped-off
      shoots.
⁶They shall all be left to the mountain
    vultures
    and to the beasts of the earth;
The vultures shall summer on them,
    all the beasts of the earth shall winter on
      them.

⁷Then will gifts be brought to the LORD of hosts—to the place of the name of the LORD of hosts, Mount Zion—from a people tall and bronzed, from a people dreaded near and far, a nation strong and conquering, whose land is washed by rivers.

continue

God will protect Jerusalem (see also Pss 46, 48)—a belief that gave shape to his ministry.

The Gospels use this same metaphor centuries later when they testify to Christian belief in the divinity of Jesus. Jesus calms the Sea of Galilee and his disciples marvel at his power asking, "What sort of man is this, whom even the winds and the sea obey?" (Matt 8:27).

18:1–19:25 Against Egypt

The two Israelite kingdoms were sandwiched between Egypt and the Mesopotamian Empires. The goal of the latter was the conquest of Egypt, command of its resources, and control over the trade routes between Egypt and Mesopotamia. Egypt, of course, resisted, and the Israelite kingdoms were caught in the crossfire. There was a particularly destructive escalation of this crossfire in 714 B.C. The Assyrians were poised on the border of Egypt, ready to invade. Egypt wanted a buffer between it and the Assyrian army so it encouraged several Assyrian vassal states in the eastern Mediterranean region to revolt and reassert their independence. What the prophet suggests is that Judah keep away from any such activity.

The prophet was certain that Judah could maintain its political independence if it learned to trust God rather than to engage in futile political and military machinations. It was an open secret that Egypt and Ethiopia were conspiring against the aggression of Assyria. The prophet believed that God determines the course of events—the plans that people make are worthless. God will bring about an end to the Assyrian Empire, but it will come when God chooses. What Judah must do is wait for a sign that God will begin to move against the Assyrians. The victory that God will effect will lead the conspirators to Jerusalem to bring tribute to Judah's God. What Judah must do is wait.

The prophet then becomes specific as he describes some of the signs of God's dominion over Egypt. The first of these are the internal divisions in Egypt that make possible the rise of a new pharaoh (the "cruel master" and "harsh king" of 19:4). The new king that the prophet speaks of is likely Piankhi, the founder

CHAPTER 19

Egypt

¹Oracle on Egypt:
See, the LORD is riding on a swift cloud
    on his way to Egypt;
The idols of Egypt tremble before him,
    the hearts of the Egyptians melt within
        them.
²I will stir up Egypt against Egypt:
    brother will war against brother,
Neighbor against neighbor,
    city against city, kingdom against kingdom.
³The courage of the Egyptians shall ebb away
        within them,
    and I will bring their counsel to nought;
They shall consult idols and charmers, ghosts
        and clairvoyants.
⁴I will deliver Egypt
    into the power of a cruel master,
A harsh king who shall rule over them—
    oracle of the Lord, the LORD of hosts.
⁵The waters shall be drained from the sea,
    the river shall parch and dry up;
⁶Its streams shall become foul,
    and the canals of Egypt shall dwindle and
        parch.
Reeds and rushes shall wither away,
    ⁷and bulrushes on the bank of the Nile;
All the sown land along the Nile
    shall dry up and blow away, and be no more.
⁸The fishermen shall mourn and lament,
    all who cast hook in the Nile;
Those who spread their nets in the water
    shall pine away.

⁹The linen-workers shall be disappointed,
    the combers and weavers shall turn pale;
¹⁰The spinners shall be crushed,
    all the hired laborers shall be despondent.
¹¹Utter fools are the princes of Zoan!
    the wisest of Pharaoh's advisers give
        stupid counsel.
How can you say to Pharaoh,
    "I am a descendant of wise men, of
        ancient kings"?
¹²Where then are your wise men?
    Let them tell you and make known
What the LORD of hosts has planned
    against Egypt.
¹³The princes of Zoan have become fools,
    the princes of Memphis have been deceived.
The chiefs of its tribes
    have led Egypt astray.
¹⁴The LORD has prepared among them
    a spirit of dizziness,
And they have made Egypt stagger in
    whatever she does,
    as a drunkard staggers in his vomit.
¹⁵Egypt shall accomplish nothing—
    neither head nor tail, palm branch nor
        reed, shall accomplish anything.

¹⁶On that day the Egyptians shall be like women, trembling with fear, because of the LORD of hosts shaking his fist at them. ¹⁷And the land of Judah shall be a terror to the Egyptians. Every time they think of Judah, they shall stand in dread because of the plan the LORD of hosts has in mind for them.
¹⁸On that day there shall be five cities in the land of Egypt that speak the language of Canaan

continue

of the twenty-fifth dynasty. This Nubian monarch took the throne of Egypt around 714 B.C. and united Egypt, Nubia, and Ethiopia under his rule. An even more serious manifestation of divine power will come when the Nile dries up. The Egyptian economy will collapse because of this disaster. Of course, Egypt's political and economic problems make it an unreliable ally.

Despite these internal difficulties, the pharaoh's advisors urged him to become involved in international politics. Isaiah had little use for the counselors who advised the king of Judah (5:18-25), and he had no respect for the sages of Egypt, even though these sages had a reputation for wisdom. Their advice is necessarily flawed because they do not take into ac-

and swear by the LORD of hosts; one shall be called "City of the Sun."

¹⁹On that day there shall be an altar to the LORD at the center of Egypt, and a sacred pillar to the LORD near its boundary. ²⁰This will be a sign and witness to the LORD of hosts in the land of Egypt, so that when they cry out to the LORD because of their oppressors, he will send them a savior to defend and deliver them. ²¹The LORD shall make himself known to Egypt, and the Egyptians shall know the LORD in that day; they shall offer sacrifices and oblations, make vows to the LORD and fulfill them. ²²Although the LORD shall smite Egypt severely, he shall heal them; they shall turn to the LORD and he shall be moved by their entreaty and heal them.

²³On that day there shall be a highway from Egypt to Assyria; the Assyrians shall enter Egypt, and the Egyptians enter Assyria, and the Egyptians shall worship with the Assyrians.

²⁴On that day Israel shall be a third party with Egypt and Assyria, a blessing in the midst of the earth, ²⁵when the LORD of hosts gives this blessing: "Blessed be my people Egypt, and the work of my hands Assyria, and my heritage, Israel."

count the judgment of Judah's God on their country. Egypt's political and military leaders will be making decisions based on flawed advice, and these decisions will have disastrous consequences for Egypt and for its allies.

One goal of the Assyrian Empire was to bring Egypt and its wealth under Assyrian control. The two Israelite kingdoms were merely stepping-stones on the way to the real prize. Here the prophet transforms that grand strategy by making Israel the linchpin that will join Egypt and Assyria. These two bitter rivals will find themselves allied in the worship of Israel's God. Again, the prophet is carried away by his own rhetoric and describes a vision that has never been realized.

EXPLORING LESSON THREE

1. When had the Israelites previously sung a similar song of thanksgiving as that found in 12:1-6? (See Exod 15:1-4.) What themes do these songs share in common?

_____

_____

_____

_____

_____

2. Isaiah 12 celebrates what God has done and will do for Jerusalem. What experiences in your life have prompted you to "[s]ing praise to the LORD" for the gifts, guidance, or grace God has given to you? How does this praising influence the way you understand God's activity in your past, present, and future?

_____

_____

_____

_____

_____

3. Isaiah speaks of the "day of the LORD" (13:6). How do other prophets understand this day (Joel 2:1-2; Amos 5:18-20; Zeph 1:7-8)?

_____

_____

_____

_____

_____

4. Who does the commentary identify as the one "fallen from the heavens" (14:12), and how did this figure come to be identified with Satan in Christian history? (See Luke 10:18.)

_____

_____

_____

_____

_____

5. a) What mourning rituals are identified in 15:2-3?

_____

_____

_____

_____

   b) What mourning rituals are commonly observed within your family or your faith
      community?

_____

_____

_____

_____

6. What are the historical circumstances that are behind Isaiah linking the fate of Damascus
   (Aram) with that of Ephraim (the northern kingdom of Israel) in 17:3? (See Isa 7:1–8:4.)

_____

_____

_____

_____

_____

7. According to the commentary, what connection is there between Isaiah 17:12-13 and Jesus'
   calming of the storm in Matthew 8:23-27?

_____

_____

_____

_____

_____

8. Even amid oracles of doom, Isaiah speaks of the nations turning to the Lord (18:7). Do you
   believe that conversion is possible even for the most wayward? Why or why not? (See Jer
   18:7-8.)

_____

_____

_____

_____

9. a) Why was Isaiah's vision of Israel as the linchpin of unity between Egypt and Assyria so extraordinary (19:23-25)?

_____

_____

_____

_____

   b) What vision of unity among contentious nations would be equally remarkable today?

_____

_____

_____

_____

10. The commentary states that many modern readers find the "oracles against the nations" (beginning with Isa 13) difficult to read. What were your feelings as you read them?

_____

_____

_____

_____

_____

CLOSING PRAYER

Prayer

*Sing praise to the L*ORD *for he has done*
  glorious things;
  let this be known throughout all the earth.

(Isa 12:5)

Save us, Lord, from the pessimism that so often clouds our minds and the fears that wound our hearts. Help us to be more aware of the beauty of your creation, the goodness that dwells in the hearts of those we meet, and the consolation to be found in our faith in you. Loosen our tongues so we may praise you for your many gifts, especially . . .

LESSON FOUR

Isaiah 20–27

Begin your personal study and group discussion with a simple and sincere prayer such as:

Prayer

Heavenly Father, as we read the words of your prophet Isaiah, help us respond to his call to repentance and a new way of life. May our study inspire us to imitate you, the pillar of justice and the fountain of all mercy.

Read the Bible text of Isaiah 20–27 found in the outside columns of pages 68–81, highlighting what stands out to you.

Read the accompanying commentary to add to your understanding.

Respond to the questions on pages 82–84, Exploring Lesson Four.

The Closing Prayer on page 85 is for your personal use and may be used at the end of group discussion.

CHAPTER 20

Isaiah's Warning Against Trust in Egypt and Ethiopia

¹In the year the general sent by Sargon, king of Assyria, came to Ashdod, fought against it, and captured it—²at that time the LORD had spoken through Isaiah, the son of Amoz: Go and take off the sackcloth from your waist, and remove the sandals from your feet. This he did, walking naked and barefoot. ³Then the LORD said: Just as my servant Isaiah has gone naked and barefoot for three years as a sign and portent against Egypt and Ethiopia, ⁴so shall the king of Assyria lead away captives from Egypt, and exiles from Ethiopia, young and old, naked and barefoot, with buttocks uncovered, the shame of Egypt. ⁵They shall be dismayed and ashamed because of Ethiopia, their hope, and because of Egypt, their boast. ⁶The inhabitants of this coastland shall say on that day, "See what has happened to those we hoped in, to whom we fled for help and deliverance from the king of Assyria! What escape is there for us now?"

continue

20:1-6 A dramatic gesture

The prophets tried to persuade people not only with their eloquence but also with their actions. The dramatic gesture became an important part of the prophetic repertoire. Hosea married a prostitute (Hos 1–3). Jeremiah purchased land during the Babylonian siege of Jerusalem (32:1-44). Ezekiel kept silence for seven and one-half years (Ezek 3:26; 24:26-27; 33:21-22). Eclipsing them all was Isaiah's three-year period of nudity. The purpose of this gesture was to dramatize the futility of the anti-Assyrian machinations encouraged by Egypt. The prophet wanted everyone to see what would happen to the Egyptians when Assyria moved against them: they will be carried off into slavery without any clothes to cover their shame.

The Egyptians encouraged the Philistine city-state of Ashdod, which was located on the Mediterranean coast twenty-nine miles south of Jaffa, to rebel against the Assyrians. The territory of Ashdod became incorporated into the Assyrian provincial system in 734 B.C. When Sargon II came to put down the rebellion with overwhelming force, the Egyptians thought the better of challenging him and simply abandoned Ashdod to its fate. The city fell to the Assyrian army in 713 B.C. While Isaiah's advice to Judah was sound, Assyria never conquered Egypt.

21:1-10 Against Babylon

This second oracle against Babylon repeats the message of 13:1–14:22. The title of this oracle is enigmatic. The Greek suggests that the title should read: "An oracle roaring like whirlwinds in the Negev. . . . " The prophet describes the fall of Babylon. Elam and Media to the east of Babylon are preparing to engulf the ancient Near East in a new wave on conquest. The conqueror will itself be conquered. Everything is in place. The great battle is about to begin. In verses 6-10, the scene shifts. The prophet, like a sentry, is scanning the horizon for a messenger bringing news of Babylon's defeat. Finally the messenger comes: "Fallen, fallen is Babylon!" The prophet's words are confirmed by events. The implication is that the reader can have confidence in Judah's prophets.

John of Revelation cites the cry to the messenger who proclaims the fall of Babylon to the prophet (21:9; Rev 14:8; 18:2) to assert his faith in the triumph of Christ and the church over Rome and its emperor.

21:11-12 Against Edom

The prophet returns to the anti-Assyrian revolt encouraged by Egypt and led by Ashdod. Edom was an active participant in that revolt. "Dumah" may be a poetic name for Edom, which came to be known as Idumea in the Greek and Roman periods. This short oracle implies that there will be some respite from Assyrian pressure ("Morning has come"), but that it will be followed by a new round of oppression ("and again night").

21:13-17 Against Arabia

After speaking about Edom's future, the prophet turns his attention to Kedar, an association of Arabian tribes living to the east of Edom. That the prophet singles Kedar out for words of judgment shows they were a significant military

CHAPTER 21

Fall of Babylon

¹Oracle on the wastelands by the sea:
Like whirlwinds sweeping through the Negeb,
 it comes from the desert,
 from the fearful land.
²A harsh vision has been announced to me:
 "The traitor betrays,
 the despoiler spoils.
Go up, O Elam; besiege, O Media;
 put an end to all its groaning!"
³Therefore my loins are filled with anguish,
 pangs have seized me like those of a
 woman in labor;
I am too bewildered to hear,
 too dismayed to look.
⁴My mind reels,
 shuddering assails me;
The twilight I yearned for
 he has turned into dread.

continue

Isaiah's vision of the fall of Babylon

⁵They set the table,
spread out the rugs;
they eat, they drink.
Rise up, O princes,
oil the shield!
⁶For thus my Lord said to me:
Go, station a watchman,
let him tell what he sees.
⁷If he sees a chariot,
a pair of horses,
Someone riding a donkey,
someone riding a camel,
Then let him pay heed,
very close heed.
⁸Then the watchman cried,
"On the watchtower, my Lord,
I stand constantly by day;
And I stay at my post
through all the watches of the night.
⁹Here he comes—
a single chariot,
a pair of horses—
He calls out and says,
'Fallen, fallen is Babylon!
All the images of her gods
are smashed to the ground!'"
¹⁰To you, who have been threshed,
beaten on my threshing floor,
What I have heard
from the LORD of hosts,
The God of Israel,
I have announced to you.

Dumah

¹¹Oracle on Dumah:
They call to me from Seir,
"Watchman, how much longer the night?
Watchman, how much longer the night?"
¹²The watchman replies,
"Morning has come, and again night.
If you will ask, ask; come back again."

In the Steppe

¹³Oracle: in the steppe:
In the thicket in the steppe you will spend
the night,
caravans of Dedanites.
¹⁴Meet the thirsty, bring them water,
inhabitants of the land of Tema,
greet the fugitives with bread.
¹⁵For they have fled from the sword,
from the drawn sword;
From the taut bow,
from the thick of battle.

¹⁶For thus the Lord has said to me: In another year, like the years of a hired laborer, all the glory of Kedar shall come to an end. ¹⁷Few of Kedar's stalwart archers shall remain, for the LORD, the God of Israel, has spoken.

CHAPTER 22

The Valley of Vision

¹Oracle on the Valley of Vision:

force, as is confirmed by Assyrian and Babylonian sources. Isaiah announces an end of Kedar's "glory." The prophet wants to impress the people of Judah with the futility of military adventures. This was an important message for the first readers of the book of Isaiah, since Judah had no military power at all. From the prophet's perspective, this did not matter. It was Judah's commitment to justice that was decisive. It was not the Judahite state that would secure Jerusalem's future but a community founded on a just social and economic order.

22:1-14 Against Jerusalem

The prophet was not finished with his comments on the fallout from the failed revolt against Assyria led by Ashdod. Judah did not join the conspirators, so when Sargon II led his army from Assyria to Ashdod, he bypassed Jerusalem. The city's people celebrated. Isaiah

What is the matter with you now, that you
    have gone up,
    all of you, to the housetops,
²You who were full of noise,
    tumultuous city,
    exultant town?
Your slain are not slain with the sword,
    nor killed in battle.
³All your leaders fled away together,
    they were captured without use of bow;
All who were found were captured together,
    though they had fled afar off.
⁴That is why I say: Turn away from me,
    let me weep bitterly;
Do not try to comfort me
    for the ruin of the daughter of my people.
⁵It is a day of panic, rout and confusion,
    from the Lord, the GOD of hosts, in the
        Valley of Vision
Walls crash;
    a cry for help to the mountains.
⁶Elam takes up the quiver,
    Aram mounts the horses
    and Kir uncovers the shields.
⁷Your choice valleys are filled with chariots,
    horses are posted at the gates—
⁸and shelter over Judah is removed.

On that day you looked to the weapons in the House of the Forest; ⁹you saw that the breaches in the City of David were many; you collected the water of the lower pool. ¹⁰You numbered the houses of Jerusalem, tearing some down to strengthen the wall; ¹¹you made a reservoir between the two walls for the water of the old pool. But you did not look to the city's Maker, nor consider the one who fashioned it long ago.

¹²On that day the Lord,
    the GOD of hosts, called
For weeping and mourning,
    for shaving the head and wearing
        sackcloth.
¹³But look! instead, there was celebration
    and joy,
    slaughtering cattle and butchering sheep,
Eating meat and drinking wine:
    "Eat and drink, for tomorrow we die!"

¹⁴This message was revealed in my hearing from the LORD of hosts:

    This iniquity will not be forgiven you
        until you die,
    says the Lord, the GOD of hosts.

continue

regarded their response to be inappropriate since God's "beloved people" still faced divine judgment. Indeed, judgment was coming because the people of means were guilty of conspicuous consumption—seemingly unmoved by the prophet's warnings. Mercenaries from Elam and Kir will turn the city's "choice valleys" into highways for an invasion. Though the city will prepare itself for this invasion, these efforts will provide no real security because God is the one planning the city's judgment while its foolish citizens are celebrating their apparent deliverance. Jerusalem, however, will not escape judgment because it has not responded to the prophet's call for justice.

Paul quotes the words of the people of Jerusalem in verse 13 when writing about the significance of the resurrection from the dead. The apostle asserts that without belief in the resurrection, people would think only of their pleasure (1 Cor 15:32).

 The **"House of the Forest"** (22:8) is a reference to the armory built by Solomon after he finished the construction of his own palace (see 1 Kgs 7:1-5; 10:16-21). The building was so named because it was constructed with cedar beams and columns. In addition to serving as an armory, the House of the Forest also may have been used as a treasury.

71

Shebna and Eliakim

¹⁵Thus says the Lord, the GOD of hosts:
Up, go to that official,
Shebna, master of the palace,
¹⁶"What have you here? Whom have you here,
that you have hewn for yourself a tomb here,
Hewing a tomb on high,
carving a resting place in the rock?"
¹⁷The LORD shall hurl you down headlong,
mortal man!
He shall grip you firmly,
¹⁸And roll you up and toss you like a ball
into a broad land.
There you will die, there with the chariots
you glory in,
you disgrace to your master's house!
¹⁹I will thrust you from your office
and pull you down from your station.
²⁰On that day I will summon my servant
Eliakim, son of Hilkiah;
²¹I will clothe him with your robe,
gird him with your sash,
confer on him your authority.
He shall be a father to the inhabitants of
Jerusalem,
and to the house of Judah.
²²I will place the key of the House of David
on his shoulder;
what he opens, no one will shut,
what he shuts, no one will open.
²³I will fix him as a peg in a firm place,
a seat of honor for his ancestral house;
²⁴On him shall hang all the glory of his
ancestral house:
descendants and offspring,
all the little dishes, from bowls to jugs.

²⁵On that day, says the LORD of hosts, the peg
fixed in a firm place shall give way, break off and
fall, and the weight that hung on it shall be done
away with; for the LORD has spoken.

continue

22:15-25 Against Shebna and Eliakim

The prophet lays the blame for Jerusalem's folly on its leaders for the most part. Here he singles out two royal counselors for particular criticism. Shebna was King Hezekiah's chief of staff. Isaiah saw the impressive tomb that Shebna was preparing for himself. This prompted the prophet to speak about Shebna's certain fall from power. He likely advised Hezekiah to become involved in the anti-Assyrian revolt led by Ashdod. Fortunately for Judah, Hezekiah did not take Shebna's advice and demoted him (36:3). His place as chief of staff was taken by Eliakim. Isaiah expected great things from Eliakim though he too proved to be a disappointment (22:25). Those in a position to bring significant change to Judahite society did nothing to disrupt the economic status quo. They believed that their political and military maneuvering would provide Judah with security. One goal of the prophet's mission was to convince Judah of just the opposite. Only a society based on justice—one that seeks the welfare of the poor—would survive.

The book of Revelation uses the imagery of verse 22 in speaking about Christ to the church of Philadelphia (Rev 3:7).

23:1-18 Against Tyre and Sidon

Tyre and Sidon were commercial centers located on the seacoast north of ancient Israel. Their merchant ships plied the Mediterranean Sea, going as far as Tarshish, located in what is now Spain. By being efficient conduits for international trade, these cities enriched themselves. Their economic resources made them attractive prey for the aggressive Assyrian Empire. The oracles against these cities are intertwined, as was their ultimate fate. The oracle against Sidon (23:1-4, 12-14) asserts that this city would no longer profit from the grain it transported from Egypt to the rest of the ancient Near East. The prophet also proclaims that Tyre will experience divine judgment but for a limited period. Tyre will rise again, but its wealth will be dedicated to the Lord, so that it might support "those who dwell before the LORD." This flight of prophetic fancy is consistent with Isaiah's

CHAPTER 23

Tyre and Sidon

¹Oracle on Tyre:
Wail, ships of Tarshish,
  for your port is destroyed;
From the land of the Kittim
  the news reaches them.
²Silence! you who dwell on the coast,
  you merchants of Sidon,
Whose messengers crossed the sea
  ³over the deep waters,
Whose revenue was the grain of Shihor, the
  harvest of the Nile,
  you who were the merchant among the
  nations.
⁴Be ashamed, Sidon, fortress on the sea,
  for the sea has spoken,
"I have not been in labor, nor given birth,
  nor raised young men,
  nor reared young women."
⁵When the report reaches Egypt
they shall be in anguish at the report
  about Tyre.
⁶Pass over to Tarshish,
  wail, you who dwell on the coast!
⁷Is this your exultant city,
  whose origin is from old,
Whose feet have taken her
  to dwell in distant lands?
⁸Who has planned such a thing
  against Tyre, the bestower of crowns,
Whose merchants are princes,
  whose traders are the earth's honored men?
⁹The LORD of hosts has planned it,
  to disgrace the height of all beauty,
  to degrade all the honored of the earth.
¹⁰Cross to your own land,
  ship of Tarshish;
  the harbor is no more.
¹¹His hand he stretches out over the sea,
  he shakes kingdoms;
The LORD commanded the destruction
  of Canaan's strongholds:

continue

---

view of wealth: it is to be shared with those in need rather than being hoarded by the wealthy.

 The **"land of the Chaldeans"** (23:13) is a reference to the first Babylonian empire, conquered by Assyria in 729 B.C. It was the second or Neo-Babylonian Empire that would regain its independence a century later and replace Assyria as the dominant power in the ancient Middle East (see maps on pp. 11 and 12).

When Jesus condemns the cities of Capernaum, Bethsaida, and Chorazin for their failure to respond to his preaching, he says that the judgment on Tyre and Sidon will be easier than the judgment on them. It is likely that the evangelists were thinking of this oracle against the two Phoenician cities (Matt 11:21-22; Luke 10:13-14).

 A city on the Mediterranean coast of Canaan, **Tyre** was founded in the third millennium B.C. Under the leadership of Ethbaal I (887–855 B.C.), Tyre was joined with Sidon, another coastal city, to form a single political unit. The Bible identifies Ethbaal as the father of Jezebel, who promoted the worship of Baal in the kingdom of Israel during the reign of her husband, King Ahab (1 Kgs 16:31). Tyre was a leading maritime power in the eastern Mediterranean, and references to it by both Isaiah and Ezekiel bear witness to the city's enduring commercial importance (e.g., Ezek 27).

¹²Crushed, you shall exult no more,
    virgin daughter Sidon.
Arise, pass over to the Kittim,
    even there you shall find no rest.
¹³Look at the land of the Chaldeans,
    the people that has ceased to be.
Assyria founded it for ships,
    raised its towers,
Only to tear down its palaces,
    and turn it into a ruin.
¹⁴Lament, ships of Tarshish,
    for your stronghold is destroyed.

¹⁵On that day, Tyre shall be forgotten for seventy years, the lifetime of one king. At the end of seventy years, the song about the prostitute will be Tyre's song:

¹⁶Take a harp, go about the city,
    forgotten prostitute;
Pluck the strings skillfully, sing many songs,
    that you may be remembered.

¹⁷At the end of the seventy years the LORD shall visit Tyre. She shall return to her hire and serve as prostitute with all the world's kingdoms on the face of the earth. ¹⁸But her merchandise and her hire shall be sacred to the LORD. It shall not be stored up or laid away; instead, her merchandise shall belong to those who dwell before the LORD, to eat their fill and clothe themselves in choice attire.

CHAPTER 24

Judgment upon the World and the Lord's Enthronement on Mount Zion

¹See! The LORD is about to empty the earth and lay it waste;
    he will twist its surface,
    and scatter its inhabitants:
²People and priest shall fare alike:
    servant and master,
Maid and mistress,
    buyer and seller,
Lender and borrower,
    creditor and debtor.

continue

24:1-23 Judgment upon the whole earth

The oracles of judgment that the prophet utters against the nations of the ancient Near East—including Judah—provide the setting for more general prophecies of a universal judgment that follow in chapters 24–27. In these chapters, the prophet is far less specific and far more pessimistic than in chapters 13–23. Still, the prophet's pessimism is not total. While he speaks about the desolation that comes with divine judgment upon a world without justice, he does hope for a decisive manifestation of divine power that will remake the world into a place where justice triumphs. Readers will be tempted to find precise referents for the nonspecific images that these chapters contain. For example, is the city that the prophet mentions in verses 10-13 Babylon, Nineveh, Jerusalem, or Samaria? The most plausible answer is that the city is any city and every city founded on injustice and oppression. The nonspecific character of the prophet's words disengages them from a particular time and place and makes their appropriation by readers today easier. On the other hand, the vague generalities of these chapters challenge the reader's attention as the prophet tries to draw a picture of what lies ahead not simply for Babylon, Jerusalem, and Egypt but for the whole world.

Chapters 24–27 have been sometimes called the "Isaiah Apocalypse." They do contain images and motifs that later apocalyptic texts develop. While chapters 24–27 are not full-blown apocalypses, they do share with later apocalyptic texts such as Daniel 7–12 and Revelation the absolute conviction of God's sovereign rule over all creation. They look forward to its coming and await God's final triumph over the power of evil.

The first oracle (24:1-6) envisions the devastation of the earth. All people will be caught up in the destruction that will take place. Those of high social and economic status will find that their wealth will not save them, and those of a lower class will not be exempt from the evil that will come upon all. The prophet gives no specific reason for this universal judgment except for universal disobedience. Only a few people will survive.

³The earth shall be utterly laid waste, utterly
  stripped,
    for the LORD has decreed this word.
⁴The earth mourns and fades,
  the world languishes and fades;
    both heaven and earth languish.
⁵The earth is polluted because of its
  inhabitants,
    for they have transgressed laws, violated
    statutes,
      broken the ancient covenant.
⁶Therefore a curse devours the earth,
  and its inhabitants pay for their guilt;
Therefore they who dwell on earth have
  dwindled,
    and only a few are left.
⁷The new wine mourns, the vine languishes,
  all the merry-hearted groan.
⁸Stilled are the cheerful timbrels,
  ended the shouts of the jubilant,
    stilled the cheerful harp.
⁹They no longer drink wine and sing;
  strong brew is bitter to those who drink it.
¹⁰Broken down is the city of chaos,
  every house is shut against entry.
¹¹In the streets they cry out for lack of wine;
  all joy has grown dim,
    cheer is exiled from the land.

¹²In the city nothing remains but desolation,
  gates battered into ruins.
¹³For thus it shall be in the midst of the earth,
  among the peoples,
As when an olive tree has been beaten,
  as with a gleaning when the vintage is done.
¹⁴These shall lift up their voice,
  they shall sing for joy in the majesty of the
    LORD,
  they shall shout from the western sea:
¹⁵"Therefore, in the east
  give glory to the LORD!
In the coastlands of the sea,
  to the name of the LORD, the God of
    Israel!"
¹⁶From the end of the earth we hear songs:
  "Splendor to the Just One!"
But I said, "I am wasted, wasted away.
  Woe is me! The traitors betray;
    with treachery have the traitors betrayed!
¹⁷Terror, pit, and trap
  for you, inhabitant of the earth!
¹⁸One who flees at the sound of terror
  will fall into the pit;
One who climbs out of the pit
  will be caught in the trap.
For the windows on high are open
  and the foundations of the earth shake.

continue

This universal judgment will make it impossible for wine to gladden people's hearts—so terrible will be the earth's fate. Carefree hilarity will be replaced by cries of desperation. Still, when judgment comes people will be moved to praise God's righteousness (24:14-16). The theme of universal judgment is picked up again in verses 16b-23. Isaiah sees earthquakes, storms, and astronomical events as the means of divine judgment. Some early Jewish interpreters understood "the host of the heavens" (24:21) to refer to rebellious angels, though this is not explicit here. Most people in the ancient world thought that heavenly bodies were manifestations of deities (see Zeph 1:5; Jer 19:13), so personifying them as "the host of the heavens" (24:21) is something to be expected. The judgment, when it comes, will reveal the power of Judah's God, who will reign in Jerusalem. Human beings are responsible for the coming judgment, but the ultimate purpose of that judgment is not vindictiveness. Its ultimate purpose is to reveal to all the world the justice of God. The prophet envisions the end of the age with God reigning in Jerusalem "in the sight of the elders" (24:23). The book of Revelation sees God's throne sounded by those "twenty-four elders" (Rev 4:4).

¹⁹The earth will burst asunder,
  the earth will be shaken apart,
  the earth will be convulsed.
²⁰The earth will reel like a drunkard,
  sway like a hut;
Its rebellion will weigh it down;
  it will fall, never to rise again."
²¹On that day the LORD will punish
  the host of the heavens in the heavens,
  and the kings of the earth on the earth.
²²They will be gathered together
  like prisoners into a pit;
They will be shut up in a dungeon,
  and after many days they will be punished.
²³Then the moon will blush
  and the sun be ashamed,
For the LORD of hosts will reign
  on Mount Zion and in Jerusalem,
  glorious in the sight of the elders.

CHAPTER 25

*Praise for God's Deliverance and the
Celebration in Zion*

¹O LORD, you are my God,
  I extol you, I praise your name;
For you have carried out your wonderful
    plans of old,
  faithful and true.

²For you have made the city a heap,
  the fortified city a ruin,
The castle of the insolent, a city no more,
  not ever to be rebuilt.
³Therefore a strong people will honor you,
  ruthless nations will fear you.
⁴For you have been a refuge to the poor,
  a refuge to the needy in their distress;
Shelter from the rain,
  shade from the heat.
When the blast of the ruthless was like a
    winter rain,
  ⁵the roar of strangers like heat in the
    desert,
You subdued the heat with the shade of a
    cloud,
  the rain of the tyrants was vanquished.
⁶On this mountain the LORD of hosts
  will provide for all peoples
A feast of rich food and choice wines,
  juicy, rich food and pure, choice wines.
⁷On this mountain he will destroy
  the veil that veils all peoples,
The web that is woven over all nations.
  ⁸He will destroy death forever.
The Lord GOD will wipe away
  the tears from all faces;
The reproach of his people he will remove

continue

25:1-5 A prayer of thanksgiving

This hymn thanks God for a victory over a powerful but unnamed enemy. This victory is another instance of God's marvelous acts on Israel's behalf—acts that stretch back to the distant past. The enemy's capital has been destroyed, leading that "strong people" to recognize the power of Israel's God—a power that was unleashed to protect a helpless Israel. The enemy came upon Israel as an east wind off the desert whose withering heat brings crop failure, famine, and starvation in its wake. God's presence was like a cloud that protected people from the terrible heat of the terrible east wind.

Those protected by God are the "poor" and the "needy." Apocalyptic texts usually address people who consider themselves to be victims of political, social, or economic oppression. It gives their struggles meaning by assuring them that God will take their side against their oppressors. This prayer thanks God for doing just that.

25:6-10a The Lord's feast

Eating sparingly with little variation in diet was the rule for most people in the ancient world. Little wonder then that a lavish banquet became a potent symbol of the restoration of God's rule on the earth (see also Joel 2:24-26;

4:18; Ezra 3:13; Matt 22:1-10; Luke 14:15-24).
What is significant about this passage is its assertion that "all nations" will share in that banquet since God will lift the veil that obscures
the vision of the nations, bringing an end to
that which keeps Israel and the nations apart.
They will recognize Israel as God's people. It
will be as if death itself were overcome. Here
the prophet's words have a double meaning
that escapes most readers today. The Canaanite
god of the underworld was Mot, whose name
is the Hebrew word for "death." Mot was
locked in a continuous battle with Baal, the god
of fertility. When the prophet asserts that the
Lord will destroy death forever, he implies that
in the new age there will be no lack of fertility.
Hunger will no longer be a threat. People will
not have to eat sparingly. This text does not
imply that the dead will rise. What it does suggest is that God will make life worth living.
Israel will be able to acclaim its God as savior
since it is only by the power of God that all this
has happened. It is God's doing.

When Paul proclaims God's victory over the
power of death (1 Cor 15:54-55), he sees this victory as the fulfillment of Scripture. Though his
citations are free and not ascribed to a specific
book, it is likely that Paul had verse 8 in mind.
The book of Revelation also finds inspiration in
the prophet's assertion that God "will wipe
away the tears from all faces" (25:8; Rev 7:17).

25:10b-12 Against Moab

The reader's attention is drawn back to the
motif of verses 1-5: God's victory over the
powerful. Here Moab is the symbol of Israel's
powerful enemies. God will frustrate its de-
signs on Israel and it will experience a devastating defeat. This short oracle clashes with what
just preceded. In 25:6-8, God will invite all nations to the feast. Once again Israel's attitude
toward other people is shaped less by its vision
of the future and more by its experience.

26:1-6 The song of the redeemed

When the prophet dreams about the future,
his dreams are cast in patterns that try to rees-
tablish Israel in the service of the God who

from the whole earth; for the LORD has
      spoken.
⁹On that day it will be said:
"Indeed, this is our God; we looked to him,
      and he saved us!
This is the LORD to whom we looked;
      let us rejoice and be glad that he has saved
      us!"

Judgment on Moab

¹⁰For the hand of the LORD will rest on this
      mountain,
      but Moab will be trodden down
      as straw is trodden down in the mire.
¹¹He will spread out his hands in its midst,
      as a swimmer spreads out his hands to
      swim;
His pride will be brought low
      despite his strokes.
¹²The high-walled fortress he will raze,
      bringing it low, leveling it to the ground,
      to the very dust.

CHAPTER 26

Judah's Praise and Prayer for Deliverance

¹On that day this song shall be sung in the land
of Judah:

"A strong city have we;
      he sets up victory as our walls and
            ramparts.
²Open up the gates
      that a righteous nation may enter,
      one that keeps faith.
³With firm purpose you maintain peace;
      in peace, because of our trust in you."
⁴Trust in the LORD forever!
      For the LORD is an eternal Rock.
⁵He humbles those who dwell on high,
      the lofty city he brings down,
Brings it down to the ground,
      levels it to the dust.
⁶The feet of the needy trample on it—
      the feet of the poor.

continue

⁷The way of the just is smooth;
   the path of the just you make level.
⁸The course of your judgments, LORD, we
      await;
   your name and your memory are the
      desire of our souls.
⁹My soul yearns for you at night,
   yes, my spirit within me seeks you at dawn;
When your judgment comes upon the earth,
   the world's inhabitants learn justice.
¹⁰The wicked, when spared, do not learn
      justice;
   in an upright land they act perversely,
   and do not see the majesty of the LORD.
¹¹LORD, your hand is raised high,
   but they do not perceive it;
Let them be put to shame when they see
      your zeal for your people:
   let the fire prepared for your enemies
      consume them.
¹²LORD, you will decree peace for us,
   for you have accomplished all we have
      done.
¹³LORD, our God, lords other than you have
      ruled us;
   only because of you can we call upon your
      name.
¹⁴Dead they are, they cannot live,
   shades that cannot rise;
Indeed, you have punished and destroyed
      them,
   and wiped out all memory of them.

continue

enclose the faithful. The key to the victory was the people's trust in God on whom Judah must always depend. It will be those least able who will seal Judah's victories. Victory will come to the lowly, who will enter the city as victors who have been made such by the power of God alone. The poor and the lowly have no power in the present age, but the future will bring these people total victory over their oppressors.

26:7-19 A psalm celebrating victory

For the prophet, the key to Judah's future was its confidence in its God. The prophet keeps returning to that theme. Military and political realities, of course, made any other source of hope a delusion. The prayer begins by lifting up God's justice and affirms that the righteous may have confidence in it. The wicked, however, never grasp the significance of God's action in the world. The prophet prays that one day they might recognize the meaning of what God will accomplish for Judah. God will bring peace and security for Judah, but its enemies will face destruction. The letter to the Hebrews quotes verse 11 to assure its readers that judgment is coming on those who do not persevere in the faith (Heb 10:27).

 The theme of **divine punishment as a means of discipline** (26:16) is common in the Old Testament. An analogy is often suggested between God's punishments and those administered by a loving parent whose desire is to discipline and restore a rebellious child (e.g., Deut 8:5; Prov 3:11-12). God's discipline is thus presented as a sign of divine compassion and evidence of God's longing for those who have erred to return to him (Sir 18:13-14).

takes the side of the poor against the powerful. This is precisely the imagery behind the prophet's "song of the redeemed." The vision celebrated in this song foresees a future in which the fortunes of the present will be reversed: the mighty will be brought low. The prophet looks toward a time when all Judah will sing a song of victory to God. That song will celebrate Jerusalem—its walls and gates that have withstood the enemy but which welcome and

Because the promised peace has not come, the just turn to God in their distress. God's people face a very difficult time. It is like the agony of a woman in labor, but at the end of that agony, there is life. The prophet prays that there will be life for Judah. His vision of the future and the ultimate redemption of Judah shapes his attitude toward the present difficulties that the just face. That vision helps the just make sense out of the apparent contradictions of their lives. In his confidence, the prophet prays that Judah's dead also share in God's victory. Is the prophet getting carried away with his rhetoric again, or is verse 19 an expression of faith in the resurrection of the dead? It is difficult to say, but, at the very least, this text provided support for those who held that belief in years to come.

It is generally agreed that **the resurrection of the dead** (26:19) is a concept largely absent from the Old Testament, which at times seems quite emphatic that death is final (Job 7:9; Ps 89:48-49; Eccl 3:18-20). In the centuries just prior to the ministry of Jesus, however, clear belief in the resurrection of the dead made an appearance in Scripture (e.g., Dan 12:2; 2 Macc 7:9, 23). In the book of Wisdom (first century B.C.), it is only the wicked who believe that human existence ends with death; God created human beings "to be imperishable"; and the "righteousness" of those who conform themselves to God's law is "undying" (1:15; 2:1-2, 23).

26:20–27:1 The coming judgment

Though the prophet is confident about Judah's future, his attention is drawn to the dire military and political circumstances that it faced. There is death all around, but soon God will reverse Judah's fortunes by destroying those nations allied against it. Giving advice reminiscent of the story of the first Passover (Exod 12), the prophet warns his readers to shut their door until death passes them by.

To express his confidence in God's victory over every evil power, the prophet uses imagery that was ancient but never loses its power to move people. The Canaanites envisioned the creation of the world as following the defeat

¹⁵You have increased the nation, LORD,
    you have increased the nation, have added
        to your glory,
    you have extended far all the boundaries
        of the land.
¹⁶LORD, oppressed by your punishment,
    we cried out in anguish under your
        discipline.
¹⁷As a woman about to give birth
    writhes and cries out in pain,
    so were we before you, LORD.
¹⁸We conceived and writhed in pain,
    giving birth only to wind;
Salvation we have not achieved for the earth,
    no inhabitants for the world were born.
¹⁹But your dead shall live, their corpses shall
    rise!
    Awake and sing, you who lie in the dust!
For your dew is a dew of light,
    and you cause the land of shades to give
        birth.

The Lord's Response

²⁰Go, my people, enter your chambers,
    and close the doors behind you;
Hide yourselves for a brief moment,
    until the wrath is past.
²¹See, the LORD goes forth from his place,
    to punish the wickedness of the earth's
        inhabitants;
The earth will reveal the blood shed upon it,
    and no longer conceal the slain.

CHAPTER 27

The Judgment and Deliverance of Israel

¹On that day,
The LORD will punish with his sword
    that is cruel, great, and strong,
Leviathan the fleeing serpent,
    Leviathan the coiled serpent;
    he will slay the dragon in the sea.

continue

²On that day—
The pleasant vineyard, sing about it!
³I, the LORD, am its keeper,
I water it every moment;
Lest anyone harm it,
night and day I guard it.
⁴I am not angry.
But if I were to find briers and thorns,
In battle I would march against it;
I would burn it all.
⁵But if it holds fast to my refuge,
it shall have peace with me;
it shall have peace with me.

⁶In days to come Jacob shall take root,
Israel shall sprout and blossom,
covering all the world with fruit.
⁷Was he smitten as his smiter was smitten?
Was he slain as his slayer was slain?
⁸Driving out and expelling, he struggled
against it,
carrying it off with his cruel wind on a
day of storm.
⁹This, then, shall be the expiation of Jacob's
guilt,
this the result of removing his sin:
He shall pulverize all the stones of the altars
like pieces of chalk;
no asherahs or incense altars shall stand.
¹⁰For the fortified city shall be desolate,
an abandoned pasture, a forsaken
wilderness;
There calves shall graze, there they shall lie
down,
and consume its branches.
¹¹When its boughs wither, they shall be
broken off;
and women shall come to kindle fires
with them.
For this is not an understanding people;
therefore their maker shall not spare them;
their creator shall not be gracious to them.

continue

of a great sea monster that the prophet calls Leviathan. While the Canaanites believed that the decisive defeat of Leviathan took place in the past, leading to the creation of this world, the prophet asserts that this battle has yet to take place. However, he is certain that God will be victorious. Hundreds of years later, the book of Revelation uses similar imagery of a monster from the sea to speak of God's final victory over the power of evil (Rev 13:1).

27:2-6 The Lord's vineyard

The vision of God's final victory over the power of evil leads to another prayer of confidence. The prophet takes up the imagery of 5:1-7 to speak not about God's judgment on the unproductive vineyard that is Israel but about the productivity of that vineyard that is under God's protection. The fruit from the Lord's vineyard will fill "all the world." Thus the prophet again sounds a note of universalism that will be an important dimension in section four of the book.

27:7-11 The end of idolatry

Israel's salvation will take place because Israel will finally leave the worship of other gods behind. It will recognize that it is the Lord who gives the land its fertility and that it makes no sense to worship other deities. Finally, Israel is faithful to its God alone because God has removed every trace of false worship just as the withering east wind dries up every blade of grass that it touches. Once God delivers Israel, now freed from serving other gods, its enemies will face defeat and destruction.

27:12-13 Israel's restoration

God will pass in judgment one final time over the land of Israel promised to Abraham (see Gen 15:18). The Lord will traverse the full extent of that land from north to south, separating the wicked from the faithful as threshers separate grain from chaff. When that has taken place, the restoration will begin. A trumpet will sound to gather Israel, as happens for every solemn assembly (see Num 10:2-10). This time Israel in exile will assemble to worship God in Jerusalem. Thus the second section of the book of Isaiah ends like the first—with the people of Israel worshiping the Lord, their ancestral God, in Jerusalem.

> [12]On that day,
> The LORD shall beat out grain
>   from the channel of the Euphrates to the
>   Wadi of Egypt,
>   and you shall be gleaned one by one,
>   children of Israel.
> [13]On that day,
> A great trumpet shall blow,
>   and the lost in the land of Assyria
>   and the outcasts in the land of Egypt
> Shall come and worship the LORD
>   on the holy mountain, in Jerusalem.

Lesson Four

EXPLORING LESSON FOUR

1. a) What "dramatic gesture" did Isaiah perform for three years before the people of Judah, and what purpose did it serve (20:1-2)? How have other prophets used similar gestures to communicate God's message? (See Jer 32:1-44; Ezek 4:1-6; Hos 1:1-9.)

_____

_____

_____

_____

_____

b) Have you ever witnessed a religious leader or someone else engage in some kind of symbolic action? If so, what did it communicate? Was it effective?

_____

_____

_____

_____

_____

2. What great empire of later history does the book of Revelation refer to as Babylon, also proclaiming, "Fallen, fallen is Babylon" (21:9; see Rev 14:8; 18:2)? Why is the name "Babylon" especially appropriate for that empire?

_____

_____

_____

_____

_____

3. Why was it wrong for Jerusalem to rejoice at having avoided being attacked by Assyrian forces (22:1-14)?

_____

_____

_____

_____

_____

4. What city is the prophecy in 24:10-13 levied against? How might this passage in Isaiah apply to our world today?

_____

_____

_____

_____

_____

5. What works of mercy and justice have you witnessed that have inspired you to give thanks to God, as Isaiah does in 25:1-5?

_____

_____

_____

_____

_____

6. a) Why was feasting such a potent symbol of God's renewed rule over the earth (25:6)?

_____

_____

_____

_____

   b) What special meals with friends or loved ones can you look back on as special encounters with God's love and care?

_____

_____

_____

7. How important is the promise in 25:7-9 to your own faith life? (See 1 Cor 15:26, 54-55; 2 Tim 1:10.)

_____

_____

_____

_____

_____

8. Isaiah and other biblical writers sometimes describe God as a disciplinarian who punishes in order to correct and restore (26:16; see also Deut 8:5; Prov 3:11-12; Sir 18:13-14). Do you find this analogy helpful, harmful, or both?

_____

_____

_____

_____

_____

9. a) How does the image of going behind closed doors and hiding from wrath recall the first Passover (26:20-21; Exod 12:21-23)?

_____

_____

_____

_____

   b) Why would recalling Israel's exodus from Egypt be of great importance while Israel is being harshly punished?

_____

_____

_____

_____

CLOSING PRAYER

Look at the land of the Chaldeans,
  the people that has ceased to be.
Assyria founded it for ships,
  raised its towers,
Only to tear down its palaces,
  and turn it into a ruin.   (Isa 23:13)

Lord our God, how often we are tempted to put our trust in the things of this world, only to find them fade and disappoint, wither and turn to ash. May your Spirit lead us to fix our gaze not on what the world values but on those the world often forgets: the poor and the sick, the stranger and the oppressed, the lonely and the dying. With your help we promise to serve you by serving those you love. Today we pray for those most in need of our love and care, especially . . .

LESSON FIVE

Isaiah 28–32

Begin your personal study and group discussion with a simple and sincere prayer such as:

Prayer

Heavenly Father, as we read the words of your prophet Isaiah, help us respond to his call to repentance and a new way of life. May our study inspire us to imitate you, the pillar of justice and the fountain of all mercy.

Read the Bible text of Isaiah 28–32 found in the outside columns of pages 88–100, highlighting what stands out to you.

Read the accompanying commentary to add to your understanding.

Respond to the questions on pages 101–103, Exploring Lesson Five.

The Closing Prayer on page 104 is for your personal use and may be used at the end of group discussion.

CHAPTER 28

The Fate of Samaria

¹Ah! majestic garland
  of the drunkards of Ephraim,
Fading blooms of his glorious beauty,
  at the head of the fertile valley,
  upon those stupefied with wine.
²See, the LORD has a strong one, a mighty one,
  who, like an onslaught of hail, a
      destructive storm,
Like a flood of water, great and overflowing,
  levels to the ground with violence;
³With feet that will trample
  the majestic garland of the drunkards of
    Ephraim.
⁴The fading blooms of his glorious beauty
  at the head of the fertile valley
Will be like an early fig before summer:
  whoever sees it,
  swallows it as soon as it is in hand.

continue

JERUSALEM'S JUDGMENT AND SALVATION

Isaiah 28:1–39:8

The third section of the book of Isaiah is a series of literary diptychs, one side of which describes divine judgment on the two Israelite kingdoms in general and the city of Jerusalem in particular. The second side of the diptych assures the people of Jerusalem that there is a future beyond judgment. Sometimes this assurance takes the form of an oracle against one of Judah's enemies; other times the prophet proclaims an oracle of salvation for Jerusalem. The final four chapters of this section (Isa 36–39) are narratives taken almost verbatim from 2 Kings 18:13–20:19. But even they replicate this alternation between judgment and salvation. Jerusalem is threatened by the Assyrians and then miraculously saved from their power. Similarly, Hezekiah faces imminent death, but at the last moment his life is spared. But this section ends with the ominous words of the prophet Isaiah, who tells Hezekiah that Babylon will bring an end to Judah's dynasty and state.

28:1-4 The proud crown

As was the case with the two previous sections of the book, this third section begins with an oracle of judgment. This time it is directed at the arrogance of the northern kingdom of Israel. The prophet uses several metaphors in announcing divine judgment on the northern kingdom—here called Ephraim after one of its principal regions. The northern kingdom was blessed with natural beauty and agriculturally valuable land. Isaiah proclaims that its excesses have finally caught up with Ephraim. Its capital, Samaria, was a beautiful city perched on the top of a mountain. The prophet is certain that it is going to fall to its enemies. The prophet compares the city to the wilting blossoms on the crown of a merrymaker after a night of drinking. Like that garland, the city has outlived its usefulness. A storm is coming that will overwhelm it. Assyrian kings on military expeditions often compared themselves to the fury of a storm that would destroy all that stood in its path. Finally, the prophet speaks of Samaria as an early ripening fig, especially attractive to passers-by since late summer is the usual time for figs. The reason for Ephraim's predicament is the extravagance of the wealthy. They enjoy lavish meals while those who actually produced the food were living on the subsistence level with barely enough to eat. Isaiah believes that Assyria, God's chosen instrument of judgment, will make short work of Samaria and its proud crown.

28:5-6 A glorious crown

The word of judgment is followed by a word of hope that takes up the image of the crown from the previous unit. The proud crown that is Samaria is contrasted with the "glorious crown" that is the Lord. The former is facing judgment; the latter brings salvation for the remnant that will survive God's judgment on Israel. The remnant is composed of those who believe that there is a future in Zion despite the disasters that threaten.

28:7-13 Against priest and prophet

The prophet indicts the priests and prophets of his day. They fail in their appointed tasks because they are usually drunk. Here the prophet links his specific criticism with the more general indictment in 28:1. Leviticus 10:8-11 forbids

⁵On that day the LORD of hosts
   will be a glorious crown
And a brilliant diadem
   for the remnant of his people,
⁶A spirit of judgment
   for the one who sits in judgment,
And strength for those
   who turn back the battle at the gate.

Against Judah

⁷But these also stagger from wine
   and stumble from strong drink:
Priest and prophet stagger from strong drink,
   overpowered by wine;
They are confused by strong drink,
   they stagger in their visions,
   they totter when giving judgment.
⁸Yes, all the tables
   are covered with vomit,
   with filth, and no place left clean.
⁹"To whom would he impart knowledge?
To whom would he convey the message?

continue

Chapters 28–33 of Isaiah are a collection of **seemingly unrelated oracles** (prophecies), but three themes predominate: (1) condemnation of Assyria; (2) the folly of alliance with Egypt; and (3) hope for Zion's repentance and restoration. The sections are set off by the exclamation "Ah!" (Hebrew, *hoy*) or "See!" (Hebrew, *hinneh* or *hen*).

28:1-29	Judgment against Samaria (1-4) with hope (5-6); judgment against Judah (7-27) with hope (28-29)
29:1-14	Judgment against Jerusalem (1-6, 11-14); hope for deliverance (7-8)
29:15-24	Redemption of the lowly
30:1-26	Folly of alliance with Egypt (1-17); deliverance of Zion (18-26)
30:27-33	Judgment against Assyria
31:1-9	Folly of alliance with Egypt and hope for Zion
32:1-20	Hope for a just kingdom (1-8, 15-20); disaster for the complacent (9-14)
33:1-24	Judgment against Assyria (1); prayer for God's deliverance of Zion (2-9); God's response; destruction of Assyria; the new Jerusalem (10-24)

To those just weaned from milk,
  those weaned from the breast?
¹⁰For he says,
'Command on command, command on
    command,
  rule on rule, rule on rule,
  here a little, there a little!'"
¹¹Yes, with stammering lips and in a strange
    language
  he will speak to this people,
¹²to whom he said:
"This is the resting place,
  give rest to the weary;
And this is the place of repose"—
  but they refused to hear.
¹³So for them the word of the LORD shall be:
  "Command on command, command on
    command,
Rule on rule, rule on rule,
  here a little, there a little!"
So that when they walk, they shall stumble
    backward,
  broken, ensnared, and captured.
¹⁴Therefore, hear the word of the LORD, you
    scoffers,
  who rule this people in Jerusalem:
¹⁵You have declared, "We have made a
    covenant with death,
  with Sheol we have made a pact;
When the raging flood passes through,
  it will not reach us;
For we have made lies our refuge,
  and in falsehood we have found a hiding
    place,"—
¹⁶Therefore, thus says the Lord GOD:
  See, I am laying a stone in Zion,
  a stone that has been tested,
A precious cornerstone as a sure foundation;
  whoever puts faith in it will not waver.
¹⁷I will make judgment a measuring line,
  and justice a level.—
Hail shall sweep away the refuge of lies,
  and waters shall flood the hiding place.
¹⁸Your covenant with death shall be canceled

continue

priests on duty to drink. In their drunken state, Israel's religious leaders babble like infants. The quotation of the advice given by Israel's inebriated priests (28:10b) is a succession of nonsense syllables in Hebrew, though the NABRE obscures this. Similarly for those who have rejected Isaiah's indictment of their infidelity, the word of God has become a succession of nonsense syllables. What awaits them is a tragic end. Paul certainly thought of this passage when he was speaking about "the gift of tongues." He freely cites verses 11-12 in 1 Corinthians 14:21-22, although he incorrectly states that the text is from the torah.

28:14-22 Against Jerusalem's political leaders

The actions of Jerusalem's leaders to forestall the inevitable are nothing but a pact with death. Again, the prophet is playing on the name of a Canaanite deity, Mot, the god of the netherworld, whose name means death and whose activity endangers the fertility of the land (see 25:8). Jerusalem's political leaders believe that their leadership will safeguard their city's future, but actually they are only hastening its fall—its death.

The only way that Jerusalem can have any future is if it establishes a just economic system. Trying to protect the city through alliances amounts to little more than suicide. A violent rainstorm that undermined hastily built fortifications around the city gave the prophet the occasion to speak about the solid foundation that God was preparing for the city's future. This foundation is justice. While it is true that Jerusalem was dependent on God's presence in the city, God's presence was, in turn, dependent on the behavior of the city's people—in particular Jerusalem's political leaders. They, however, have not fostered justice—quite the opposite. This has left God no choice but to begin an "urban renewal project" in the city. The project had to begin with demolition so that the city could be built on the solid foundation of a just economic system.

Jerusalem's leaders believed that strong fortifications would provide all the security the city needed. Isaiah sees devastation ahead since the city will be without the effective protection that justice provides. The prophet stipulates that in the past God fought for Israel against its enemies, the Canaanites (see Josh 10:7-14) and the Philistines (see 2 Sam 5:17-25). But in the coming conflict with Assyria, God will fight against Judah and Jerusalem, something Isaiah characterizes as a "strange deed." There is time to forestall this disaster if the city changes its attitude toward the prophet's message.

At the conclusion of the parable of the Vineyard (Matt 21:33-46), Jesus makes a statement made up of several Old Testament verses strung together to explain the negative reaction to his ministry as a divine necessity. Among those verses is 28:16.

The architectural metaphor of a foundation stone or **cornerstone** is used by Isaiah to symbolize the trustworthiness of God's promises and the need to respond to those promises with faith (28:16). Jesus' reference to the rejection of "the cornerstone" in Matthew 21:42 references both Isaiah 28:16 and Psalm 118:22. In Psalms, the cornerstone may be the foundation stone of the temple. This imagery is repeated several times in the New Testament, where the cornerstone is Jesus Christ (Luke 20:17; Acts 4:11; Rom 9:33; 1 Pet 2:7).

28:23-29 A parable on judgment

Here the prophet uses a succession of rhetorical questions to underscore his message. The judgment that Jerusalem is facing will happen because God acts at the right time for the right purpose. Plowing and planting take place during specific and limited periods according to a plan. Similarly, activities connected with the harvest follow a pattern. The message is clear: all that will happen to Jerusalem will happen at God's discretion for a good reason. Another implication of the parable is that the farmer's various activities, while necessary,

and your pact with Sheol shall not stand.
When the raging flood passes through,
    you shall be beaten down by it.
¹⁹Whenever it passes, it shall seize you;
    morning after morning it shall pass,
    by day and by night.
Sheer terror
    to impart the message!
²⁰For the bed shall be too short to stretch out in,
    and the cover too narrow to wrap in.
²¹For the LORD shall rise up as on Mount Perazim,
    bestir himself as in the Valley of Gibeon,
To carry out his work—strange his work!
    to perform his deed—alien his deed!
²²Now, cease scoffing,
    lest your bonds be tightened,
For I have heard a decree of destruction
    from the Lord, the GOD of hosts,
    for the whole land.

The Parable of the Farmer

²³Give ear and hear my voice,
    pay attention and hear my word:
²⁴Is the plowman forever plowing in order to sow,
    always loosening and harrowing the field?
²⁵When he has leveled the surface,
    does he not scatter caraway and sow cumin,
Put in wheat and barley,
    with spelt as its border?
²⁶His God has taught him this rule,
    he has instructed him.
²⁷For caraway is not threshed with a sledge,
    nor does a cartwheel roll over cumin.
But caraway is beaten out with a staff,
    and cumin with a rod.
²⁸Grain is crushed for bread, but not forever;
    though he thresh it thoroughly,
    and drive his cartwheel and horses over it,
    he does not pulverize it.
²⁹This too comes from the LORD of hosts;
    wonderful is his counsel and great his wisdom.

continue

CHAPTER 29

Judgment and Deliverance of Jerusalem

¹Ah! Ariel, Ariel,
　city where David encamped!
Let year follow year,
　and feast follow feast,
²But I will bring distress upon Ariel,
　and there will be mourning and moaning.
You shall be to me like Ariel:
　³I will encamp like David against you;
I will circle you with outposts
　and set up siege works against you.
⁴You shall speak from beneath the earth,
　and from the dust below, your words shall
　　come.
Your voice shall be that of a ghost from the
　earth,
　and your words shall whisper from the
　　dust.
⁵The horde of your arrogant shall be like fine
　dust,
　a horde of tyrants like flying chaff.
Then suddenly, in an instant,
　⁶you shall be visited by the LORD of hosts,
With thunder, earthquake, and great noise,
　whirlwind, storm, and the flame of
　　consuming fire.
⁷Then like a dream,
　a vision of the night,
Shall be the horde of all the nations
　who make war against Ariel:
All the outposts, the siege works against it,
　all who distress it.
⁸As when a hungry man dreams he is eating
　and awakens with an empty stomach,

continue

have a limited duration so Jerusalem's judgment will be of limited duration as well. While divine judgment is coming, it is not God's final word to Jerusalem.

29:1-8 Jerusalem's judgment and salvation

Isaiah addresses Jerusalem as "Ariel," a name whose significance is unclear. This Hebrew word simply does not occur often enough in the Bible to be sure about its meaning. Ezekiel uses this word to speak of the place of sacrifice, the "altar hearth" where offerings are burnt (Ezek 43:15). If Isaiah understands Ariel in the same way, the prophet may intend this word to imply that Jerusalem will be the setting for the forthcoming sacrifice of Judah's leaders and people. The literal meaning of Ariel is "the lion of God," but the significance of that meaning in this context is also not obvious.

The opening verse of the oracle suggests that the New Year's celebration provided the prophet with an opportunity to speak about what lay ahead for the city. Isaiah declares that a hostile army will surround the city. This siege will lead the people to raise a great lamentation, which will fail to move God since God is intent on making a sacrifice of the city. But the nations chosen to place Jerusalem on the altar of sacrifice will not escape divine judgment. This will not save Jerusalem, but the nations arrayed against it will be judged for their failures as well. Still, the judgment of these nations is a sign of Jerusalem's restoration. Jesus' lament over Jerusalem uses the language and imagery of the prophet's oracle against Ariel (29:3; Luke 19:43).

 The reference to David encamped before Jerusalem (29:3) recalls **the siege of Jerusalem by David** and his army, which was followed by their defeat of the Jebusites and seizure of the city (2 Sam 5:6-10).

29:9-16 Against the sages

The prophet, who has already criticized some of Israel's leadership (28:7-22), turns his attention to Jerusalem's sages. He probably has in mind the royal counselors rather than the wise and prudent elders that people sought out for their advice. Like the rest of Jerusalem's leadership, the sages are not fulfilling their responsibilities. The contribution to Judah is as effective as that of a drunk, but they were not drunk with wine like the priests and prophet. They are unable to provide sound advice because God has made it impossible for them to see Jerusalem's true status before God. It is as if all their skill has left them. The prophet blames this on the people of Jerusalem who are content with merely going through the motions during worship. Worst of all, the sages approach the crisis Jerusalem was facing as if it should be handled by diplomatic maneuvering. They do not recognize that the city's future is in God's hands—not theirs. Jesus quotes verse 13 when he criticizes the religious observance of some of his contemporaries (Matt 15:8; Mark 7:6-7). Paul cites verse 16 to affirm the justice of God (Rom 9:21).

The image of **God as a potter** (29:16) appears also in Sirach 33:13 and Jeremiah 18:1-10. As in Isaiah, Sirach uses the image to emphasize that God decides the fates of human beings in accordance with the divine will. Jeremiah makes use of the image in a similar way but on a larger scale, comparing the potter's ability to keep or discard the clay vessels he has made with God's sovereignty in shaping the fates of nations.

Or when a thirsty man dreams he is drinking
  and awakens faint, his throat parched,
So shall the horde of all the nations be,
  who make war against Mount Zion.

Blindness and Perversity

[9]Stupefy yourselves and stay stupid;
  blind yourselves and stay blind!
You who are drunk, but not from wine,
  who stagger, but not from strong drink!
[10]For the LORD has poured out on you
  a spirit of deep sleep.
He has shut your eyes (the prophets)
  and covered your heads (the seers).

[11]For you the vision of all this has become like the words of a sealed scroll. When it is handed to one who can read, with the request, "Read this," the reply is, "I cannot, because it is sealed." [12]When the scroll is handed to one who cannot read, with the request, "Read this," the reply is, "I cannot read."

  [13]The Lord said:
Since this people draws near with words only
  and honors me with their lips alone,
  though their hearts are far from me,
And fear of me has become
  mere precept of human teaching,
[14]Therefore I will again deal with this people
  in surprising and wondrous fashion:
The wisdom of the wise shall perish,
  the prudence of the prudent shall vanish.
[15]Ah! You who would hide a plan
  too deep for the LORD!
Who work in the dark, saying,
  "Who sees us, who knows us?"
[16]Your perversity is as though the potter
  were taken to be the clay:
As though what is made should say of its
    maker,
  "He did not make me!"
Or the vessel should say of the potter,
  "He does not understand."

continue

Redemption

¹⁷Surely, in a very little while,
  Lebanon shall be changed into an
    orchard,
  and the orchard be considered a forest!
¹⁸On that day the deaf shall hear
    the words of a scroll;
And out of gloom and darkness,
    the eyes of the blind shall see.
¹⁹The lowly shall again find joy in the LORD,
    the poorest rejoice in the Holy One of
      Israel.
²⁰For the tyrant shall be no more,
    the scoffer shall cease to be;
All who are ready for evil shall be cut off,
    ²¹those who condemn with a mere word,
Who ensnare the defender at the gate,
    and leave the just with an empty claim.
²²Therefore thus says the LORD,
    the God of the house of Jacob,
    who redeemed Abraham:
No longer shall Jacob be ashamed,
    no longer shall his face grow pale.
²³For when his children see
    the work of my hands in his midst,
They shall sanctify my name;
    they shall sanctify the Holy One of Jacob,
    be in awe of the God of Israel.
²⁴Those who err in spirit shall acquire
      understanding,
    those who find fault shall receive
      instruction.

CHAPTER 30

*Oracle on the Futility of an Alliance
with Egypt*

¹Ah! Rebellious children,
    oracle of the LORD,
Who carry out a plan that is not mine,
    who make an alliance I did not inspire,
    thus adding sin upon sin;
²They go down to Egypt,
    without asking my counsel,

continue

29:17-24 A reversal of fortunes

The prophet looks forward to a time when Israel will have the kind of spiritual sensitivity that should mark the people of God. Unfortunately, this is still lacking. There are the devout who tried to live in accord with the divine will (the "lowly" and "poorest" of 29:19). Then there are those who led a life that was best described as godless (the arrogant "tyrant" and "scoffer" of 29:20). Finally, there is a large percentage of "Jacob's children" who are simply ignorant of God's will and promises for Israel (the "blind" and the "deaf" of 29:18). The prophet envisions a time when the latter will be healed, but he appears to intimate that the arrogant are beyond hope. For the prophet a sure sign of God's final act in favor of Israel will be the conversion and incorporation of those who are spiritually insensitive within the community of those already committed to justice.

The Bible is filled with examples of the **"reversal of fortunes"** theme, including the ascendency of Jacob over his brother Isaac (Gen 25:23), the prayer of Hannah (1 Sam 2:4-8), and the canticle of Mary (Luke 1:46-55). Certain parables and teachings of Jesus are based on a reversal of fortune, such as the parable of the workers in the vineyard in Matthew 20:1-16. (See also Matt 19:30; Mark 10:31, 44.)

The social and economic disparity between the poor and the arrogant was serious and it could not go on for much longer. The prophet believed that a reversal of fortunes was coming. God was about to act on behalf of those who were being oppressed. The lowly and poor will find joy, while the arrogant will have gone. When the devout see God's actions on their behalf, their faith will be confirmed and they will be led to an ever greater fidelity to God, for they will stand in awe of God's holiness. The most significant outcome of God's action on behalf of the poor will be the effect it will have on those who "err in spirit" and "find fault." Those people who drag down the spirit of Israel will

To seek strength in Pharaoh's protection
  and take refuge in Egypt's shadow.
³Pharaoh's protection shall become your
  shame,
  refuge in Egypt's shadow your disgrace.
⁴When his princes are at Zoan
  and his messengers reach Hanes,
⁵All shall be ashamed
  of a people that gain them nothing,
Neither help nor benefit,
  but only shame and reproach.
⁶Oracle on the Beasts of the Negeb.
Through the distressed and troubled land
  of the lioness and roaring lion,
  of the viper and flying saraph,
They carry their riches on the backs of donkeys
  and their treasures on the humps of camels
To a people good for nothing,
⁷to Egypt whose help is futile and vain.
Therefore I call her
  "Rahab Sit-still."
⁸Now come, write it on a tablet they can keep,
  inscribe it on a scroll;
That in time to come it may be
  an eternal witness.
⁹For this is a rebellious people,
  deceitful children,
Children who refuse
  to listen to the instruction of the LORD;
¹⁰Who say to the seers, "Do not see";
  to the prophets, "Do not prophesy truth
    for us;
  speak smooth things to us, see visions that
    deceive!

¹¹Turn aside from the way! Get out of the
    path!
  Let us hear no more
  of the Holy One of Israel!"
¹²Therefore, thus says the Holy One of Israel:
  Because you reject this word,
And put your trust in oppression and deceit,
  and depend on them,
¹³This iniquity of yours shall be
  like a descending rift
Bulging out in a high wall
  whose crash comes suddenly, in an instant,
¹⁴Crashing like a potter's jar
  smashed beyond rescue,
And among its fragments cannot be found
  a sherd to scoop fire from the hearth
  or dip water from the cistern.
¹⁵For thus said the Lord GOD,
  the Holy One of Israel:
By waiting and by calm you shall be saved,
  in quiet and in trust shall be your strength.
  But this you did not will.
¹⁶"No," you said,
  "Upon horses we will flee."
  Very well, you shall flee!
"Upon swift steeds we will ride."
  Very well, swift shall be your pursuers!
¹⁷A thousand shall tremble at the threat of
    one—
  if five threaten, you shall flee.
You will then be left like a flagstaff on a
    mountaintop,
  like a flag on a hill.

continue

be transformed and will be firmly convinced that the future belongs to the God of Israel.

30:1-17 Against a compact with Egypt

Conventional wisdom for a small state like Judah caught between two superpowers like Egypt and Assyria was to play off the superpowers against each other. Judah does just that by considering an alliance with Egypt to insure that the Assyrian threat would be neutralized. The prophet consistently advises against this conventional wisdom. Isaiah characterizes Egypt as "Rahab Sit-still." Rahab is another name for the sea monster that represents the forces of chaos, which God has already defeated (see Job 26:12). The prophet believed that by aligning itself with Egypt, Judah was setting itself up for more severe treatment from

95

Zion's Future Deliverance

[18]Truly, the LORD is waiting to be gracious to
you,
truly, he shall rise to show you mercy;
For the LORD is a God of justice:
happy are all who wait for him!
[19]Yes, people of Zion, dwelling in Jerusalem,
you shall no longer weep;
He will be most gracious to you when you
cry out;
as soon as he hears he will answer you.
[20]The Lord will give you bread in adversity
and water in affliction.
No longer will your Teacher hide himself,
but with your own eyes you shall see your
Teacher,
[21]And your ears shall hear a word behind you:
"This is the way; walk in it,"
when you would turn to the right or the
left.
[22]You shall defile your silver-plated idols
and your gold-covered images;
You shall throw them away like filthy rags,
you shall say, "Get out!"
[23]He will give rain for the seed
you sow in the ground,
And the bread that the soil produces
will be rich and abundant.
On that day your cattle will graze
in broad meadows;
[24]The oxen and the donkeys that till the
ground
will eat silage tossed to them
with shovel and pitchfork.
[25]Upon every high mountain and lofty hill
there will be streams of running water.
On the day of the great slaughter,
when the towers fall,
[26]The light of the moon will be like the light
of the sun,
and the light of the sun will be seven
times greater,
like the light of seven days,

continue

Assyria than if it simply submitted. The prophet's strategy in dealing with the Assyrian threat was for Judah to remain passive, making no overt attempts at opposing the unstoppable Assyrian army. He is convinced that the people of Judah will not escape foreign domination because God has chosen Assyria as the instrument of judgment upon Jerusalem.

Isaiah's words reflect his frustration with Judah's political leaders. They look for prophets whose words support their fatally flawed foreign policy. But Isaiah believes that God did not speak through those prophets. Judah has rejected Isaiah's message, which counseled trust in God alone—without relying on alliances, national pride, or armed resistance. The prophet, of course, has made it clear that Judah will not evade divine judgment because of the injustice in Judahite society. But he asserts that submission to Assyria will prevent the total destruction of Judah. The country's leaders, however, labored under the illusion that they could escape judgment. This was their great mistake.

30:18-26 Jerusalem's future

The prophet can envision a glorious future for Jerusalem because he believes that the city's future is not determined by its infidelity but by God's fidelity. After the city experiences God's judgment, there will come deliverance. This oracle begins by identifying the Lord as a "God of justice." The key then to the glorious future that awaits Jerusalem is a just social and economic order—not the city's supposed status as God's dwelling place on earth.

The intensity of Jerusalem's distress at the prospect of Assyrian domination should not lead it to despair but to confident assurance in the coming redemption. God will give to the people all that they need for their life and will insure that the people of Jerusalem have the kind of instruction which, when heard and applied, will keep them from deviating in any way from a life that is in accord with God's will, thus insuring the permanence of the city's deliverance.

The consequence of this new obedience will go beyond the moral order and affect nature;

the land will enjoy unparalleled fertility. The contemporary concern for the wise use of natural resources can easily resonate with the prophet's vision, which posits a connection between human righteousness and the fruitfulness of the land.

The prophet concludes by using apocalyptic imagery in speaking of Jerusalem's restoration. The light of the sun and the moon will be so increased that night will be indistinguishable from day and the daylight will be seven times more intense than in the present. When will this happen? The answer is on the day of the "great slaughter" when God will rise up against the enemies of the just and bring down the towers of their strength. In order that the faithful be not afraid of that day, the prophet concludes by describing it as a time when God will heal the wounds of the past that were endured by the just.

 Isaiah's image of **God as a healer** binding up the wounds of the people (30:26b) is a frequent biblical image. One feature that many of these images have in common is that it is God who both inflicts the wound and binds it up (see Job 5:18; Ps 147:2-3; Ezek 34:16). The image therefore contains elements that reflect both God's justice and mercy.

30:27-33 Against Assyria

For Jerusalem to live in peace, Assyria will have to fall. Here the prophet asserts that one day this mighty empire will be no more. While Isaiah teaches that God is using the militaristic and expansionist Assyrian Empire as a means to bring down Judah and its unjust social and economic system, the prophet does not endorse the policies of Assyria. Again he makes it clear that Assyria will have to answer for its own crimes. God will descend upon Assyria like a violent winter storm. Assyria will not be able to resist this divine judgment. Of course, Judah will rejoice at Assyria's fall, which is certain to come since God's judgment comes upon injustice and oppression wherever it is found.

On the day the LORD binds up the wounds
of his people
and heals the bruises left by his blows.

Divine Judgment on Assyria

²⁷See, the name of the LORD is coming from
afar,
burning with anger, heavy with threat,
His lips filled with fury,
tongue like a consuming fire,
²⁸Breath like an overflowing torrent
that reaches up to the neck!
He will winnow the nations with a
destructive winnowing
and bridle the jaws of the peoples to send
them astray.
²⁹For you, there will be singing
as on a night when a feast is observed,
And joy of heart
as when one marches along with a flute
Going to the mountain of the LORD,
to the Rock of Israel.
³⁰The LORD will make his glorious voice
heard,
and reveal his arm coming down
In raging fury and flame of consuming fire,
in tempest, and rainstorm, and hail.
³¹For at the voice of the LORD, Assyria will
be shattered,
as he strikes with the rod;
³²And every sweep of the rod of his
punishment,
which the LORD will bring down on him,
Will be accompanied by timbrels and lyres,
while he wages war against him.
³³For his tophet has long been ready,
truly it is prepared for the king;
His firepit made both deep and wide,
with fire and firewood in abundance,
And the breath of the LORD, like a stream of
sulfur,
setting it afire.

continue

CHAPTER 31

Against the Egyptian Alliance

¹Ah! Those who go down to Egypt for help,
  who rely on horses;
Who put their trust in chariots because of
      their number,
  and in horsemen because of their
      combined power,
But look not to the Holy One of Israel
  nor seek the Lord!
²Yet he too is wise and will bring disaster;
  he will not turn from his threats.
He will rise up against the house of the wicked
  and against those who help evildoers.
³The Egyptians are human beings, not God,
  their horses flesh, not spirit;
When the Lord stretches forth his hand,
  the helper shall stumble, the one helped
      shall fall,
  and both of them shall perish together.
⁴For thus says the Lord to me:
As a lion or its young
  growling over the prey,
With a band of shepherds
  assembled against it,
Is neither dismayed by their shouts
  nor cowed by their noise,
So shall the Lord of hosts come down
  to wage war upon Mount Zion, upon its
      height.
⁵Like hovering birds, so the Lord of hosts
  shall shield Jerusalem,
To shield and deliver,
  to spare and rescue.

⁶Return, O Israelites, to him whom you have
utterly deserted. ⁷On that day each one of you
shall reject his idols of silver and gold, which your
hands have made.

⁸Assyria shall fall by a sword, not wielded by
      human being,
  no mortal sword shall devour him;
He shall flee before the sword,

continue

31:1-3 Against Egypt

The prophet returns to his attempts to discourage Judah from making an alliance with Egypt against Assyria. An alliance with Egypt appeared to be the right move since Egypt could supply a formidable chariot force which could aid Judah in resisting the Assyrian invaders. Actually, Egypt's chariots would have been of limited use since most of Judah's important cities were in the central highlands where chariots were not maneuverable.

The prophet reasserts the advice he consistently gives to Judah under threat from Assyria: trust in God. God's purposes will be achieved no matter what alliances Judah may make. After all, the Egyptians are human beings and their horses are mere flesh. They could not possibly thwart the plan of God, who has determined to bring an end of Judah's political, religious, and economic institutions because of the injustice that they foster. No chariot army will be able to stop this plan.

31:4-7 God protects Jerusalem

The prophet uses two metaphors to speak of Jerusalem's deliverance. The first is clear enough. God is like a lion that will not surrender its prey though shepherds will try to frighten it off (31:4). The second is more obscure (31:5). The phrasing in the NABRE suggests that God is like birds circling overhead, protecting the city. The Hebrew is not as clear though the parallel with verse 4 suggests that the goal of this imagery is to suggest that God will not abandon Jerusalem. Still, the image of birds circling overhead suggests desolation rather than protection. Of course, this must be seen against the wider backdrop of the Isaianic tradition that affirms that Jerusalem must expect divine judgment because of its oppressive and unjust economic system. Still, the city has a future beyond judgment. What this passage affirms is that God's protection will not allow Jerusalem's total destruction at the hands of its enemies. God's deliverance of the city will finally persuade its people to recognize the claims that God has on their exclusive loyalty. The people will finally stop looking for security by serving gods other than the Lord.

31:8-9 Against Assyria

God's deliverance of Jerusalem can come only at the expense of the Assyrians. Again, the prophet affirms that the time of Assyrian power is limited. When the Assyrian Empire falls, it will be God's doing. The prophet is trying to persuade his readers that their future and the future of their city are in God's hands so they can look toward that future with confidence and assurance. Those who read these words, after the book of Isaiah achieved the shape it now has, lived many years after the Assyrian Empire had fallen to the Babylonian Empire, which, in turn, fell to the Persian Empire. The prophet's audience, however, was still looking for the complete restoration of Jerusalem. Certainly these words were meant to keep their hopes from flagging. After all, Assyria did fall as the prophet said it would. One could have confidence in the prophetic word.

32:1-8 New leadership for Jerusalem

To put a positive spin on his vision of Jerusalem's future, the prophet speaks about leadership. He assures his readers that there will come a time when the current perverse social and economic order will be set aright. Those who have the responsibility for maintaining a just social order will fulfill their responsibilities. In the prophet's day, justice was perverted. People called evil good and fools wise. The poor deserve to have justice done when they are in the right, and apparently there is no one to take their side. But it is not only the poor that suffer. Society itself is transformed into something it should not be. The prophet looks for the day when competent and just political leadership will guide the community. Note there is no hint that this political leadership will come from the Davidic dynasty.

32:9-14 Judgment on Jerusalem

The prophet again shifts his mood abruptly. After describing his vision of a just city led by competent rulers, he moves back to the harsh reality that he has experienced. He speaks to a city under judgment. He turns his attention to the women of the upper classes as he did in

and his young men shall be impressed as laborers.
[9]He shall rush past his crag in panic,
and his princes desert the standard in terror,
Says the LORD who has a fire in Zion
and a furnace in Jerusalem.

CHAPTER 32

The Kingdom of Justice

[1]See, a king will reign justly
and princes will rule rightly.
[2]Each of them will be like a shelter from the wind,
a refuge from the rain.
They will be like streams of water in a dry country,
like the shade of a great rock in a parched land.
[3]The eyes of those who see will not be closed;
the ears of those who hear will be attentive.
[4]The hasty of heart shall take thought to know,
and tongues of stutterers shall speak readily and clearly.
[5]No more will the fool be called noble,
nor the deceiver be considered honorable.
[6]For the fool speaks folly,
his heart plans evil:
Godless actions,
perverse speech against the LORD,
Letting the hungry go empty
and the thirsty without drink.
[7]The deceits of the deceiver are evil,
he plans devious schemes:
To ruin the poor with lies,
and the needy when they plead their case.
[8]But the noble plan noble deeds,
and in noble deeds they persist.

The Women of Jerusalem

[9]You women so complacent, rise up and hear my voice,

continue

99

daughters so confident, give heed to my words.

¹⁰In a little more than a year
    your confidence will be shaken;
For the vintage will fail,
    no fruit harvest will come in.
¹¹Tremble, you who are so complacent!
    Shudder, you who are so confident!
Strip yourselves bare,
    with only a loincloth for cover.
¹²Beat your breasts
    for the pleasant fields,
    for the fruitful vine;
¹³For the soil of my people,
    overgrown with thorns and briers;
For all the joyful houses,
    the exultant city.
¹⁴The castle will be forsaken,
    the noisy city deserted;
Citadel and tower will become wasteland
    forever,
    the joy of wild donkeys, the pasture of
    flocks;
¹⁵Until the spirit from on high
    is poured out on us.
And the wilderness becomes a garden land
    and the garden land seems as common as
    forest.
¹⁶Then judgment will dwell in the wilderness
    and justice abide in the garden land.
¹⁷The work of justice will be peace;
    the effect of justice, calm and security
    forever.
¹⁸My people will live in peaceful country,
    in secure dwellings and quiet resting places.
¹⁹And the forest will come down completely,
    the city will be utterly laid low.
²⁰Happy are you who sow beside every stream,
    and let the ox and the donkey go freely!

3:16–4:1, because these women were good symbols of the excesses of the wealthy. The prophet warns them that their lives of ease will come to an unexpected end very soon. They ought to be worried. A most appropriate response would be for them to adopt the attitude of mourners with the hope of engaging God's sympathy for their plight. Soon the wealthy will be mourning because their lives of extravagance will end. The soil will lose its fecundity and the cities of Judah will be deserted. The land will revert to the state before human habitation transformed it.

32:15-20 An idyllic future

As quickly as the prophet moved from vision to reality, he shifts back to a vision of an idyllic future. He is convinced that the oracle of judgment he conveyed to the women of the upper classes is not God's final word to Judah. God will send the spirit to make the earth fruitful once again. Human society will be marked by justice. Justice will make it possible for all people to have what they need to lead happy lives. The imagery that the prophet uses here appears to suggest he believes that in the future the people of Judah would be living in small villages. Again, the prophet allows his rhetoric to get the best of him. He expects Jerusalem to be restored. It will be purged of the injustices that have made it the object of divine judgment. The prophet, then, was not one who rejected city life as somehow incompatible to the ideals of traditional Israelite morality. What is essential to the prophet's vision of Judah's future is that justice will lead to peace.

EXPLORING LESSON FIVE

1. a) Isaiah describes Samaria (capital of Ephraim, or the northern kingdom of Israel) as a once magnificent garland (28:1). To what would you compare your city, state, or nation?

_____

_____

_____

_____

   b) What strengths and weaknesses do you find in the location you describe above, especially in terms of justice and care for the vulnerable?

_____

_____

_____

_____

2. Why have the priests and prophets of northern Israel (Ephraim) been unable to teach or speak a message from God (28:7-10)?

_____

_____

_____

_____

_____

3. a) How might one guard against the spiritual danger Isaiah associates with Israel's ritual worship (29:13-14)? (See Mark 7:6-7.)

_____

_____

_____

_____

   b) How do you understand true, authentic worship?

_____

_____

_____

_____

4. How do you understand the natural tension between relying upon God for all of our needs while still receiving "strength" and "protection" from people, places, and things (30:1-2)? (See Matt 6:24-34.)

_____

_____

_____

_____

_____

_____

5. What importance does "Rahab" have in the cultural world of Isaiah's time (30:7)? (See Job 9:13; 26:12; Ps 89:11.)

_____

_____

_____

_____

_____

_____

6. Isaiah describes several signs that the Lord will be gracious and will show mercy (30:18-26). What are these signs? Which of them is the most meaningful to you and why?

_____

_____

_____

_____

_____

_____

7. What animal symbols does Isaiah use for God in 31:4-5, and how do these symbols help to describe God's care for Jerusalem?

_____

_____

_____

_____

_____

8. What evils are called "[g]odless" and "deceit[ful]" in 32:6-7?

_____

_____

_____

_____

_____

_____

9. Isaiah describes a scene of devastating spiritual complacency among people who are materially well-off (32:9-14). Do these dangers persist today? In what way(s)? (See Matt 6:19-20; Luke 12:15-21.)

_____

_____

_____

_____

_____

_____

CLOSING PRAYER

Prayer

*Is the plowman forever plowing in order to sow,
    always loosening and harrowing the field?
When he has leveled the surface,
    does he not scatter caraway and sow cumin,
Put in wheat and barley,
    with spelt as its border?*   (Isa 28:24-25)

Too often, Lord, we spend our lives preparing to act but
never acting. We are like bent bows from which the
arrow never flies! And yet you want us to be your image
and presence on earth, manifesting your love and goodness to all. Move us today on your behalf to act boldly
with charity and compassion, especially as you call us
to . . .

LESSON SIX

Isaiah 33–39

Begin your personal study and group discussion with a simple and sincere prayer such as:

Prayer

> *Heavenly Father, as we read the words of your prophet Isaiah, help us respond to his call to repentance and a new way of life. May our study inspire us to imitate you, the pillar of justice and the fountain of all mercy.*

Read the Bible text of Isaiah 33–39 found in the outside columns of pages 106–116, highlighting what stands out to you.

Read the accompanying commentary to add to your understanding.

Respond to the questions on pages 117–119, Exploring Lesson Six.

The Closing Prayer on page 120 is for your personal use and may be used at the end of group discussion.

CHAPTER 33

Overthrow of Assyria

¹Ah! You destroyer never destroyed,
   betrayer never betrayed!
When you have finished destroying, you will
      be destroyed;
   when you have stopped betraying, you
      will be betrayed.
²LORD, be gracious to us; for you we wait.
   Be our strength every morning,
   our salvation in time of trouble!
³At the roaring sound, peoples flee;
   when you rise in your majesty, nations are
      scattered.
⁴Spoil is gathered up as caterpillars gather,
   an onrush like the rush of locusts.
⁵The LORD is exalted, enthroned on high;
   he fills Zion with right and justice.
⁶That which makes her seasons certain,
   her wealth, salvation, wisdom, and
      knowledge,
   is the fear of the LORD, her treasure.
⁷See, the men of Ariel cry out in the streets,
   the messengers of Shalem weep bitterly.
⁸The highways are desolate,
   travelers have quit the paths,
Covenants are broken, witnesses spurned;
   yet no one gives it a thought.
⁹The country languishes in mourning,
   Lebanon withers with shame;
Sharon is like the Arabah,
   Bashan and Carmel are stripped bare.
¹⁰Now I will rise up, says the LORD,
   now exalt myself,
   now lift myself up.
¹¹You conceive dry grass, bring forth stubble;
   my spirit shall consume you like fire.
¹²The peoples shall be burned to lime,
   thorns cut down to burn in fire.
¹³Hear, you who are far off, what I have done;
   you who are near, acknowledge my might.
¹⁴In Zion sinners are in dread,
   trembling grips the impious:

continue

33:1-16 God's justice

This chapter begins with a woe oracle against an unnamed enemy who has threatened Jerusalem—a conventional way of speaking about the city's importance for the future of God's people. The unnamed enemy is the Assyrian Empire, whose demise the prophet announces yet again. The destruction of its enemy means the glorification of Jerusalem, which occupies the prophet's attention in this oracle. That glorification comes because God will rule Jerusalem. God's rule will insure that Zion will be filled with justice and righteousness. These, of course, are prophetic code words for a just social order in which the poor find protection against the greed and arrogance of the rich. Verses 14-16 show how the prophet adapted the question-and-answer pattern of entrance liturgies (e.g., Pss 15, 24) to underscore the importance of justice in the lives of those who would be part of a restored Jerusalem.

33:17-24 A new Jerusalem

The prophet describes Jerusalem after God has removed the Assyrian threat to the city and established justice for the city's poor and oppressed. The prophet uses conventional imagery to speak about God's rule from Zion. The worship of Judah's God will take place without

"Who of us can live with consuming fire?
   who of us can live with everlasting
      flames?"
¹⁵Whoever walks righteously and speaks
   honestly,
   who spurns what is gained by oppression,
Who waves off contact with a bribe,
   who stops his ears so as not to hear of
      bloodshed,
   who closes his eyes so as not to look on
      evil—
¹⁶That one shall dwell on the heights,
   with fortresses of rock for stronghold,
   food and drink in steady supply.
¹⁷Your eyes will see a king in his splendor,
   they will look upon a vast land.
¹⁸Your mind will dwell on the terror:
   "Where is the one who counted, where
      the one who weighed?
   Where the one who counted the
      towers?"
¹⁹You shall no longer see a defiant people,
   a people of speech too obscure to
      comprehend,
   stammering in a tongue not understood.
²⁰Look to Zion, the city of our festivals;
   your eyes shall see Jerusalem
   as a quiet abode, a tent not to be struck,
Whose pegs will never be pulled up,
   nor any of its ropes severed.

²¹Indeed the Lᴏʀᴅ in majesty will be there
   for us
   a place of rivers and wide streams
   on which no galley may go,
   where no majestic ship may pass.
²²For the Lᴏʀᴅ is our judge,
   the Lᴏʀᴅ is our lawgiver,
   the Lᴏʀᴅ is our king;
   he it is who will save us.
²³The rigging hangs slack;
   it cannot hold the mast in place,
   nor keep the sail spread out.
Then the blind will divide great spoils
   and the lame will carry off the loot.
²⁴No one who dwells there will say, "I am
      sick";
   the people who live there will be forgiven
      their guilt.

CHAPTER 34

Judgment upon Edom

¹Come near, nations, and listen;
   be attentive, you peoples!
Let the earth and what fills it listen,
   the world and all it produces.
²The Lᴏʀᴅ is angry with all the nations,
   enraged against all their host;
He has placed them under the ban,
   given them up to slaughter.

continue

interruption. God's law will guide the city's government, but the prophet allows himself a little poetic license as he speaks of God's dwelling in Zion protected by "rivers and wide streams." There are no rivers or streams in the vicinity of Jerusalem. Finally, sickness and sin will be only a memory. The prophet uses this imagery to move the people to see their future as the work of God rather than the result of political maneuvering.

Isaiah 33:22 recalls an earlier period of a united Israel. During this time God's people were ruled not by a king but by divinely guided charismatic leaders, or "judges." Israel's decision to abandon this form of leadership in the time of Samuel, prophet and last of the judges, was interpreted as a rejection of **God as Israel's king** (1 Sam 8:7). In Isaiah's vision of a renewed Jerusalem, God's kingship is rightfully restored.

³Their slain shall be cast out,
their corpses shall send up a stench;
the mountains shall run with their blood,
⁴All the host of heaven shall rot;
the heavens shall be rolled up like a scroll.
All their host shall wither away,
as the leaf wilts on the vine,
or as the fig withers on the tree.
⁵When my sword has drunk its fill in the
heavens,
it shall come down upon Edom for
judgment,
upon a people under my ban.
⁶The LORD has a sword sated with blood,
greasy with fat,
With the blood of lambs and goats,
with the fat of rams' kidneys;
For the LORD has a sacrifice in Bozrah,
a great slaughter in the land of Edom.
⁷Wild oxen shall be struck down with fatlings,
and bullocks with bulls;
Their land shall be soaked with blood,
and their soil greasy with fat.
⁸For the LORD has a day of vengeance,
a year of requital for the cause of Zion.
⁹Edom's streams shall be changed into pitch,
its soil into sulfur,
and its land shall become burning pitch;
¹⁰Night and day it shall not be quenched,
its smoke shall rise forever.
From generation to generation it shall lie
waste,
never again shall anyone pass through it.
¹¹But the desert owl and hoot owl shall
possess it,
the screech owl and raven shall dwell in it.
The LORD will stretch over it the measuring
line of chaos,
the plumb line of confusion.
¹²Its nobles shall be no more,
nor shall kings be proclaimed there;
all its princes are gone.
¹³Its castles shall be overgrown with thorns,
its fortresses with thistles and briers.

continue

34:1-17 Against Edom

The prophet turns his attention to the nations again. He does not specify the crimes that the nations have committed, but he promises that God's judgment will be severe and complete. Edom is singled out for harsh judgment because of its proximity to Judah and its behavior when Jerusalem was militarily and politically impotent.

In describing the devastation that will overtake Edom at God's command, Isaiah describes the devastated countryside as populated with a variety of birds, three of which are types of **owls** (34:11). Owls are among the birds considered to be unclean according to the torah's dietary laws (Lev 11:13-18; Deut 14:12-18). More importantly, in Isaiah's day, owls were a well-known symbol of desolation and were often depicted in Scripture as inhabitants of ruins and harbingers of misfortune (Ps 102:7; Zeph 2:14).

The prophet promises the territory of Edom will become a region without human habitation. Its land will be a haunt for wild creatures once again. Edom will sink into chaos and will be little more than a bad memory for Judah. Its destruction will be as complete as that of Sodom and Gomorrah (Gen 19:24). Nothing can save Edom from its judgment.

Modern readers find the language of this oracle particularly repellant. The prophet's harshness reflects his conviction that the conflict he was describing was not simply between Judah and the nations but a conflict between God and the powers of evil that attempt to frustrate God's rule. It is not just that Assyria or Edom suffers military defeat. The heavens and their host are the opponents that God defeats. In a battle with the powers of evil, God can give no quarter. What happens to the nations is simply the terrible consequence of the conflict that went on in the heavens. The focus on Edom, of course, reflects the pressure that Edom was exerting on Judah. The exaggeration so clearly evident in the oracle is a matter of rhetorical convention and also a genuine ill will that gripped the people of Judah toward Edom.

 The **"lilith"** (34:14) is a female demon, perhaps originally of Assyrian origin, whose abode was believed to be desert places. The root of the name ultimately derives from the Sumerian word *lil*, meaning "spirit" or "wind." Later rabbinic lore speaks of Lilith as Adam's first wife.

35:1-10 Zion's joy

The contrast between this passage and the preceding oracle against Edom could not be any stronger. In the previous oracle, nature serves as the means of divine judgment with Edom's territory reverting to a wild state. Here nature is transformed to make the restoration of Jerusalem possible. In both instances, God's power accomplishes the deed. Both the judgment of Edom and the salvation of Jerusalem bring glory to God.

This imagery and the thrust of this oracle are similar to that found in the fourth section of the book, chapters 40–55. The motif of the desert's transformation in verses 1-2 recurs in 40:3; that of God's coming to save in verse 4 in 40:9-10;

It shall become an abode for jackals,
    a haunt for ostriches.
¹⁴Wildcats shall meet with desert beasts,
    satyrs shall call to one another;
There shall the lilith repose,
    and find for herself a place to rest.
¹⁵There the hoot owl shall nest and lay eggs,
    hatch them out and gather them in her
        shadow;
There shall the kites assemble,
    each with its mate.
¹⁶Search through the book of the LORD and
    read:
    not one of these shall be lacking,
For the mouth of the LORD has ordered it,
    and his spirit gathers them there.
¹⁷It is he who casts the lot for them;
    his hand measures off their portions;
They shall possess it forever,
    and dwell in it from generation to
        generation.

CHAPTER 35

Israel's Deliverance

¹The wilderness and the parched land will exult;
    the Arabah will rejoice and bloom;
²Like the crocus it shall bloom abundantly,
    and rejoice with joyful song.
The glory of Lebanon will be given to it,
    the splendor of Carmel and Sharon;
They will see the glory of the LORD,
    the splendor of our God.
³Strengthen hands that are feeble,
    make firm knees that are weak,
⁴Say to the fearful of heart:
    Be strong, do not fear!
Here is your God,
    he comes with vindication;
With divine recompense
    he comes to save you.
⁵Then the eyes of the blind shall see,
    and the ears of the deaf be opened;

continue

⁶Then the lame shall leap like a stag,
  and the mute tongue sing for joy.
For waters will burst forth in the wilderness,
  and streams in the Arabah.
⁷The burning sands will become pools,
  and the thirsty ground, springs of water;
The abode where jackals crouch
  will be a marsh for the reed and papyrus.
⁸A highway will be there,
  called the holy way;
No one unclean may pass over it,
  but it will be for his people;
  no traveler, not even fools, shall go astray
    on it.
⁹No lion shall be there,
  nor any beast of prey approach,
  nor be found.
But there the redeemed shall walk,
¹⁰And the ransomed of the LORD shall
    return,
  and enter Zion singing,
  crowned with everlasting joy;
They meet with joy and gladness,
  sorrow and mourning flee away.

CHAPTER 36

Invasion of Sennacherib

¹In the fourteenth year of King Hezekiah, Sennacherib, king of Assyria, went up against all the fortified cities of Judah and captured them. ²From Lachish the king of Assyria sent his commander with a great army to King Hezekiah in Jerusalem. When he stopped at the conduit of the upper pool, on the highway of the fuller's field, ³there came out to him the master of the palace, Eliakim, son of Hilkiah, and Shebna the scribe, and the chancellor, Joah, son of Asaph. ⁴The commander said to them, "Tell Hezekiah: Thus says the great king, the king of Assyria: On what do you base this trust of yours? ⁵Do you think mere words substitute for strategy and might in war? In whom, then, do you place your trust, that you rebel against me? ⁶Do you trust in Egypt, that

continue

the healing of the blind in verse 5 and of lame in verse 6 in 40:5 and 42:7; the miraculous highway of verse 8 in 40:3; and the disappearance of sorrow in verse 10 in 51:11. Clearly, this chapter was meant to serve as a bridge to the next section of the book. But why is this chapter placed here, before the chapters (36–39) that end the third section of the book with a historical review of the Assyrian and Babylonian crises? One possibility is that the prophet wished to emphasize that God's plans for Zion transcend history. They are not dependent upon what people do but on the sovereign act of a God who is determined to restore Jerusalem.

The transformation of the desert from an arid, life-threatening place to a fertile, life-supporting place is a common biblical image of salvation. Israel is not blessed with a river system like those in Egypt and Mesopotamia. The threat of drought followed by crop failure, famine, and starvation was always a serious threat. Speaking of God's movement in Israel's life as eliminating that threat was natural for ancient Israel's poets and theologians. The text affirms that the desert and parched lands will become like Lebanon where rains are plentiful, the Carmel range that guards the fertile Jezreel Valley, and Sharon that was a well-watered plain along the coast.

These new circumstances ought to encourage those people who were unable to see any future for themselves as God's people. Similarly, God's movement in their lives will be as miraculous as the opening of blind eyes and the loosing of a mute's tongue. Returning to the metaphor of the transformed desert in verse 7, the prophet asserts that the wilderness will no longer be a dangerous place, the haunt of lions and jackals. There will be a highway there, allowing the people of Judah to return to Jerusalem with joy. The death of Judah's political and religious institutions and the exile of its leading citizens threatened the people's very existence, but God will come with vindication and salvation.

There are at least six allusions to this text in the New Testament: 35:3 (Heb 12:12); verses 5-6 (Matt 11:5; Mark 7:37; Luke 7:22; Acts

26:18); and verse 10 (Rev 21:4). The most striking is the citing of this text by the people who witnessed Jesus' healing of a man with impaired hearing and speaking (Mark 7:37). Though the prophet composed this text to encourage Jews to hold on to their ancestral faith, the New Testament reinterprets this text to proclaim its faith in Jesus.

36:1–37:9a Jerusalem threatened

The third section of the book of Isaiah closes with a prose account of the Assyrian siege of Jerusalem that took place during the reign of Hezekiah (715–698 B.C.). The account is taken from 2 Kings 18:13–20:19 with some notable differences.

The Assyrians, led by their king Sennacherib, began their campaign in Judah by taking forty-six fortified cities. From Lachish, the last of these, Sennacherib sends his Rabshakeh (chief of staff) to Jerusalem, demanding surrender. Meeting with his Judahite counterparts, the Rabshakeh underscores the futility of resistance to the Assyrian forces arrayed against Jerusalem. He asserts that Egypt is an unreliable ally, that Hezekiah's centralization of worship in Jerusalem undermined any religious support he may have enjoyed, and that Jerusalem's fighting forces have been seriously depleted. Finally, the Assyrian asserts that he is following the command of Jerusalem's own God by attacking the city.

The Judahite negotiators are afraid that the Rabshakeh's confident assertions will undermine the morale of Jerusalem's defenders so they ask the Assyrian to speak Aramaic rather than Hebrew, in order to keep the negotiations secret from the people of Jerusalem. This, of course, the Assyrian negotiator refused to do. In fact, he spoke directly to the city's defenders, who had to face the shortages that are inevitable in any siege. The Assyrian demanded the surrender of the city, but he promised to provide an ample supply of food if the people gave up their resistance. He reminded the people of Jerusalem that the gods of many nations proved unable to save their peoples from the Assyrian onslaught, so the likelihood of the

broken reed of a staff which pierces the hand of anyone who leans on it? That is what Pharaoh, king of Egypt, is to all who trust in him. [7]Or do you say to me: It is in the LORD, our God, we trust? Is it not he whose high places and altars Hezekiah has removed, commanding Judah and Jerusalem, 'Worship before this altar'?

[8]"Now, make a wager with my lord, the king of Assyria: I will give you two thousand horses, if you are able to put riders on them. [9]How then can you turn back even a captain, one of the least servants of my lord, trusting, as you do, in Egypt for chariots and horses? [10]Did I come up to destroy this land without the LORD? The LORD himself said to me, Go up and destroy that land!"

[11]Then Eliakim and Shebna and Joah said to the commander, "Please speak to your servants in Aramaic; we understand it. Do not speak to us in the language of Judah within earshot of the people who are on the wall."

[12]But the commander replied, "Was it to your lord and to you that my lord sent me to speak these words? Was it not rather to those sitting on the wall, who, with you, will have to eat their own excrement and drink their own urine?" [13]Then the commander stepped forward and cried out in a loud voice in the language of Judah, "Listen to the words of the great king, the king of Assyria. [14]Thus says the king: Do not let Hezekiah deceive you, for he cannot rescue you. [15]And do not let Hezekiah induce you to trust in the LORD, saying, 'The LORD will surely rescue us, and this city will not be handed over to the king of Assyria.' [16]Do not listen to Hezekiah, for thus says the king of Assyria:

Make peace with me
and surrender to me!
Eat, each of you, from your vine,
each from your own fig tree.
Drink water, each from your own well,
[17]until I arrive and take you
to a land like your own,
A land of grain and wine,
a land of bread and vineyards.

continue

[18]Do not let Hezekiah seduce you by saying, 'The LORD will rescue us.' Has any of the gods of the nations rescued his land from the power of the king of Assyria? [19]Where are the gods of Hamath and Arpad? Where are the gods of Sepharvaim? Where are the gods of Samaria? Have they saved Samaria from my power? [20]Who among all the gods of these lands ever rescued their land from my power, that the LORD should save Jerusalem from my power?" [21]But they remained silent and did not answer at all, for the king's command was, "Do not answer him."

[22]Then the master of the palace, Eliakim, son of Hilkiah, Shebna the scribe, and the chancellor Joah, son of Asaph, came to Hezekiah with their garments torn, and reported to him the words of the commander.

CHAPTER 37

[1]When King Hezekiah heard this, he tore his garments, covered himself with sackcloth, and went into the house of the LORD. [2]He sent Eliakim, the master of the palace, and Shebna the scribe, and the elders of the priests, covered with sackcloth, to tell the prophet Isaiah, son of Amoz,

[3]"Thus says Hezekiah:
A day of distress and rebuke,
  a day of disgrace is this day!
Children are due to come forth,
  but the strength to give birth is lacking.

[4]Perhaps the LORD, your God, will hear the words of the commander, whom his lord, the king of Assyria, sent to taunt the living God, and will rebuke him for the words which the LORD, your God, has heard. So lift up a prayer for the remnant that is here."

[5]When the servants of King Hezekiah had come to Isaiah, [6]he said to them: "Tell this to your lord: Thus says the LORD: Do not be frightened by the words you have heard, by which the deputies of the king of Assyria have blasphemed me.

[7]I am putting in him such a spirit
  that when he hears a report

continue

Lord saving Judah is remote. The Judahite negotiators were clearly shaken as they made their report to Hezekiah.

When the Judahite negotiators consult Isaiah, he says that Sennacherib will break off the siege, return to Assyria, and be killed there. The prophet asserts that Hezekiah has nothing to fear from the Assyrian threat. When the Rabshakeh returned to Lachish, he found out that Sennacherib had left that city because he heard of Egyptian plans to move against Assyria.

One detail that this account omits from that of 2 Kings 18 is Hezekiah's submission to Sennacherib and the subsequent payment of a heavy indemnity to the Assyrian king (see 2 Kgs 18:14-16). Such action clashes with the advice the prophet gives in 37:6-7. What the Isaianic account underscores is the hopelessness of Jerusalem's situation and Isaiah's confidence in the city's eventual deliverance.

37:9b-38 Jerusalem saved

In what appears to be a parallel account of the Assyrian siege of Jerusalem, Isaiah's role is much more prominent. After receiving a letter from Sennacherib calling for the surrender of Jerusalem, Hezekiah prays that the Lord will do what the gods of the nations could not: halt the Assyrian juggernaut. The prophet responds in poetic form that Sennacherib's plans will fail because the Assyrian king has insulted the Lord. God promises that, despite Sennacherib's earlier conquests, his attempt to take Jerusalem will fail. The prophet also asserts that before Jerusalem's deliverance, it will have to suffer because the normal cultivation of crops will not take place, inducing a famine that will be relieved only after two years. Also, only a remnant of Jerusalem's population will survive this disaster.

The prose accounts end with the prophet's prediction that Sennacherib would never even invade Jerusalem because God will protect it for the sake of David. But the Assyrians did besiege the city, though they did end it and return to Assyria. The narrative underscores the miraculous nature of Jerusalem's deliverance by asserting that an "angel of the LORD" annihilated the Assyrian army in its camp. What

he will return to his land.
I will make him fall by the sword in his
land.”

[8]When the commander, on his return, heard that the king of Assyria had withdrawn from Lachish, he found him besieging Libnah. [9]The king of Assyria heard a report: “Tirhakah, king of Ethiopia, has come out to fight against you.” Again he sent messengers to Hezekiah to say: [10]“Thus shall you say to Hezekiah, king of Judah: Do not let your God in whom you trust deceive you by saying, ‘Jerusalem will not be handed over to the king of Assyria.’ [11]You, certainly, have heard what the kings of Assyria have done to all the lands: they put them under the ban! And are you to be delivered? [12]Did the gods of the nations whom my fathers destroyed deliver them—Gozan, Haran, Rezeph, and the Edenites in Telassar? [13]Where are the king of Hamath, the king of Arpad, or a king of the cities Sepharvaim, Hena or Ivvah?”

[14]Hezekiah took the letter from the hand of the messengers and read it; then he went up to the house of the LORD, and spreading it out before the LORD, [15]Hezekiah prayed to the LORD:

[16]“LORD of hosts, God of Israel,
enthroned on the cherubim!
You alone are God
over all the kingdoms of the earth.
It is you who made
the heavens and the earth.
[17]Incline your ear, LORD, and listen!
open your eyes, LORD, and see!
Hear all the words Sennacherib has sent
to taunt the living God.

[18]Truly, O LORD,
the kings of Assyria have laid waste
the nations and their lands.
[19]They gave their gods to the fire
—they were not gods at all,
but the work of human hands—
Wood and stone, they destroyed them.
[20]Therefore, LORD, our God,
save us from this man’s power,
That all the kingdoms of the earth may know
that you alone, LORD, are God.”

[21]Then Isaiah, son of Amoz, sent this message to Hezekiah: “Thus says the LORD, the God of Israel, to whom you have prayed concerning Sennacherib, king of Assyria: I have listened! [22]This is the word the LORD has spoken concerning him:

She despises you, laughs you to scorn,
the virgin daughter Zion;
Behind you she wags her head,
daughter Jerusalem.
[23]Whom have you insulted and blasphemed,
at whom have you raised your voice
And lifted up your eyes on high?
At the Holy One of Israel!
[24]Through the mouths of your messengers
you have insulted the Lord when you said:
‘With my many chariots I went up
to the tops of the peaks,
to the recesses of Lebanon,
To cut down its lofty cedars,
its choice cypresses;
I reached the farthest shelter,
the forest ranges.
[25]I myself dug wells
and drank foreign water;

continue

actually led to the end of the siege is not known for certain. Most likely Hezekiah paid a heavy price for protection (2 Kgs 18:15-16) and agreed to vassal status. This allowed Sennacherib to break off the siege and return to Assyria so that he could deal with internal unrest, which eventually ended with his assassination.

Over time, the precise circumstances of Jerusalem’s deliverance were forgotten. Of course, the city’s narrow escape came to support a belief that Jerusalem would never fall because of divine protection. One of Isaiah’s contemporaries, Micah, however, announced the city’s eventual fall (Mic 3:9-12). Still, most people began to con-

Drying up all the rivers of Egypt
    beneath the soles of my feet.'
[26]Have you not heard?
    A long time ago I prepared it,
    from days of old I planned it,
Now I have brought it about:
    You are here to reduce
    fortified cities to heaps of ruins,
[27]Their people powerless,
    dismayed and distraught,
They are plants of the field,
    green growth,
    thatch on the rooftops,
Grain scorched by the east wind.
[28]I know when you stand or sit,
    when you come or go,
    and how you rage against me.
[29]Because you rage against me
    and your smugness has reached my ears,
I will put my hook in your nose
    and my bit in your mouth,
And make you leave by the way you came.
[30]This shall be a sign for you:
This year you shall eat the aftergrowth,
    next year, what grows of itself;
But in the third year, sow and reap,
    plant vineyards and eat their fruit!
[31]The remaining survivors of the house of
    Judah
    shall again strike root below
    and bear fruit above.
[32]For out of Jerusalem shall come a remnant,
    and from Mount Zion, survivors.
The zeal of the LORD of hosts shall do this.

[33]Therefore, thus says the LORD about the
    king of Assyria:
He shall not come as far as this city,
    nor shoot there an arrow,
    nor confront it with a shield,
Nor cast up a siege-work against it.
[34]By the way he came he shall leave,
    never coming as far as this city,
    oracle of the LORD.
[35]I will shield and save this city
for my own sake and the sake of David my
    servant."

[36]Then the angel of the LORD went forth and struck down one hundred and eighty-five thousand in the Assyrian camp. Early the next morning, there they were, all those corpses, dead! [37]So Sennacherib, the king of Assyria, broke camp, departed, returned home, and stayed in Nineveh.

[38]When he was worshiping in the temple of his god Nisroch, his sons Adrammelech and Sharezer struck him down with the sword and fled into the land of Ararat. His son Esarhaddon reigned in his place.

CHAPTER 38

Sickness and Recovery of Hezekiah

[1]In those days, when Hezekiah was mortally ill, the prophet Isaiah, son of Amoz, came and said to him: "Thus says the LORD: Put your house in order, for you are about to die; you shall not recover." [2]Hezekiah turned his face to the wall and prayed to the LORD:

[3]"Ah, LORD, remember how faithfully and wholeheartedly I conducted myself in your presence, doing what was good in your sight!" And Hezekiah wept bitterly.

[4]Then the word of the LORD came to Isaiah: [5]Go, tell Hezekiah: Thus says the LORD, the God of your father David: I have heard your prayer; I have seen your tears. Now I will add fifteen years to your life. [6]I will rescue you and this city from the hand of the king of Assyria; I will be a shield to this city.

[7]This will be the sign for you from the LORD that the LORD will carry out the word he has spoken: [8]See, I will make the shadow cast by the sun on the stairway to the terrace of Ahaz go back the ten steps it has advanced. So the sun came back the ten steps it had advanced.

Hezekiah's Hymn of Thanksgiving

[9]The song of Hezekiah, king of Judah, after he had been sick and had recovered from his illness:

continue

sider it a matter of divine honor for the Lord to keep Jerusalem from all harm. About one hundred years later, Jeremiah was nearly executed for daring to suggest that God would allow Jerusalem to fall (see Jer 26:1-19).

38:1-8 Hezekiah's illness

The experience of Judah is duplicated in the experience of its king. Hezekiah faces certain death but then is spared to live for fifteen more years. The imagery of verse 38 that recounts the reversal of the sun's movement suggests that deliverance will follow upon the crisis facing both Hezekiah and Jerusalem. Of course, this deliverance is only temporary. Hezekiah will die and Jerusalem will fall.

 The **reversal of the sun's movement** (38:7-8) recalls the story of the sun standing still for Joshua's victory over the five Amorite kings (Josh 10:13). Both instances are demonstrations of God's faithfulness and absolute sovereignty over the forces of nature that God has created.

38:9-20 Hezekiah's prayer of thanksgiving

Hezekiah offers a prayer that follows the pattern of other biblical prayers that thank God for deliverance in time of personal peril, e.g., Psalms 6, 13, 22. The prayer begins with words expressing resignation. Death is coming. Though Hezekiah cries for help, he expects his end to be imminent. Still, he cries for help. He wants to live. The king realizes that his illness was a message from God that was not designed to punish but to save him. He thanks God for being rescued from sin and death. The king dedicates his life to the praise of God who saved him from death. If only Jerusalem would have responded to its deliverance in a similar fashion.

[10]In the noontime of life I said,
   I must depart!
To the gates of Sheol I have been consigned
   for the rest of my years.
[11]I said, I shall see the LORD no more
   in the land of the living.
Nor look on any mortals
   among those who dwell in the world.
[12]My dwelling, like a shepherd's tent,
   is struck down and borne away from me;
You have folded up my life, like a weaver
   who severs me from the last thread.
From morning to night you make an end
      of me;
   [13]I cry out even until the dawn.
Like a lion he breaks all my bones;
   from morning to night you make an end
      of me.
[14]Like a swallow I chirp;
   I moan like a dove.
My eyes grow weary looking heavenward:
   Lord, I am overwhelmed; go security
      for me!
[15]What am I to say or tell him?
   He is the one who has done it!
All my sleep has fled,
   because of the bitterness of my soul.
[16]Those live whom the LORD protects;
   yours is the life of my spirit.
You have given me health and restored my
      life!
   [17]Peace in place of bitterness!
You have preserved my life
   from the pit of destruction;
Behind your back
   you cast all my sins.
[18]For it is not Sheol that gives you thanks,
   nor death that praises you;
Neither do those who go down into the pit
   await your kindness.
[19]The living, the living give you thanks,
   as I do today.
Parents declare to their children,
   O God, your faithfulness.

continue

²⁰The LORD is there to save us.
  We shall play our music
In the house of the LORD
  all the days of our life.

²¹Then Isaiah said, "Bring a poultice of figs and apply it to the boil for his recovery." ²²Hezekiah asked, "What is the sign that I shall go up to the house of the LORD?"

CHAPTER 39

Embassy from Merodach-baladan

¹At that time Merodach-baladan, son of Baladan, king of Babylon, sent letters and gifts to Hezekiah, when he heard that he had been sick and had recovered. ²Hezekiah was pleased at their coming, and then showed the messengers his treasury, the silver and gold, the spices and perfumed oil, his whole armory, and everything in his storerooms; there was nothing in his house or in all his realm that Hezekiah did not show them.

³Then Isaiah the prophet came to King Hezekiah and asked him, "What did these men say to you? Where did they come from?" Hezekiah replied, "They came to me from a distant land, from Babylon." ⁴He asked, "What did they see in your house?" Hezekiah answered, "They saw everything in my house. There is nothing in my storerooms that I did not show them." ⁵Then Isaiah said to Hezekiah, "Hear the word of the LORD of hosts: ⁶The time is coming when all that is in your house, everything that your ancestors have stored up until this day, shall be carried off to Babylon; nothing shall be left, says the LORD. ⁷Some of your own descendants, your progeny, shall be taken and made attendants in the palace of the king of Babylon." ⁸Hezekiah replied to Isaiah, "The word of the LORD which you have spoken is good." For he thought, "There will be peace and stability in my lifetime."

39:1-4 The embassy from Babylon

The Babylonians wanted to topple the Assyrians from the position of dominance, so they sent an ambassador to enlist Hezekiah's cooperation in an anti-Assyrian coalition. But Judah had few resources to offer to the enterprise. Hezekiah shows his treasury to the Babylonian ambassador to make it clear how much the Assyrians required in tribute. Isaiah comes to the king to make certain he did not join the coalition, but Hezekiah assured him that all he did was show the Babylonians how little he had to offer.

39:5-8 The exile to Babylon

Of course, the prophet wants to make it clear that Judah's future does not lie with Babylon—no matter how attractive an alliance with it may appear to be. He warns the king that the Babylonians were going to strip the royal family of the little wealth it has remaining and, after doing so, lead the royals into exile where they would be servants of Babylon's kings. The king agrees with the prophet's assessment of the future but is confident that his reign will end before disaster comes upon Judah.

The book of Isaiah does not describe Jerusalem's fall to the Babylonians, though the next section (chapters 40–55) envisions Judah's restoration following the Babylonian conquest of Jerusalem, the destruction of its temple, and the exile of its leading citizens. The prophet's words to Hezekiah about the eventual fall of the city are needed to effect the transition to the next section of the book.

EXPLORING LESSON SIX

1. While "sinners" in Zion are to be in dread of God's judgment (33:14), what characterizes those who are promised blessing instead (33:15-16)?

2. Why might the promise made to Jerusalem in 33:21 be an outlandish one?

3. a) What is the "ban" that Isaiah says God has placed on the nations, particularly Edom (34:2)? (See Deut 13:13-19; Josh 6:15-21.) How does the commentary help us understand the harsh nature of this ban?

    b) What do you think Jesus would teach about this "ban"? (See Matt 5:38-48.)

4. a) How are the promises of 35:4-6a used in Matthew 11:2-6?

b) In what way might the promise of miraculous healings in Isaiah be seen as a metaphor for God's power to transform our lives?

_____

_____

_____

_____

5. Sennacherib's messenger purposely speaks in a way that is meant to demoralize the people of Jerusalem and humiliate their leaders (36:11-12). How has your faith enabled you to cope with situations in which others have sought to sow fear in your mind or embarrass you?

_____

_____

_____

_____

_____

_____

6. According to the commentary, what significant difference is there between Isaiah's account of Sennacherib's invasion of Judah (36:1–37:9a) and the nearly identical account in 2 Kings 18:13–20:19? Why might Isaiah's account (37:6-7) omit this information?

_____

_____

_____

_____

_____

7. King Hezekiah instinctively turns to God in prayer when he receives the threatening letter from the king of Assyria (37:16-20). When have you been inspired to pray for help or deliverance? How did God respond?

_____

_____

_____

_____

_____

_____

8. a) How did Sennacherib's letter to Hezekiah blaspheme the Lord (37:10-13)?

_____

_____

_____

_____

 b) How does Isaiah's prophecy in 37:22-35 counter Sennacherib's claim to invincibility? (See also John 19:10-11.)

_____

_____

_____

_____

9. Now that you have completed your study of Isaiah 1–39, what themes or images have had the most impact or meaning for you? What most disturbed you about Isaiah's prophecies? What are you looking forward to in your study of Isaiah 40–66?

_____

_____

_____

_____

_____

CLOSING PRAYER

Prayer

For the LORD is our judge,
the LORD is our lawgiver,
the LORD is our king;
he it is who will save us.   (Isa 33:22)

Free us, Lord God, from every false idol that challenges our faith in you. Banish from our hearts the empty attractions of wealth, status, comfort, and other passing pleasures and distractions. We acknowledge your loving sovereignty over our bodies and minds, our hearts and our souls. May we become more and more faithful to you by placing you at the center of all we do. As our time studying your word comes to a close, we pray for one another, especially . . .

PRAYING WITH YOUR GROUP

Because we know that the Bible allows us to hear God's voice, prayer provides the context for our study and sharing. By speaking and listening to God and each other, the discussion often grows to more deeply bond us to one another and to God.

At *the beginning and end of each lesson* simple prayers are provided for individual use, and also may be used within the group setting. Most of the closing prayers provided with each lesson relate directly to a theme from that lesson and encourage you to pray together for people and events in your local community.

Of course, there are many ways to center ourselves in God's presence as we gather together in groups around the word of God. We provide some additional suggestions here knowing you and your group will make prayer a priority as part of your gathering. These are simply alternative ways to pray if your group would like to try something different from those prayers provided in the previous pages.

Conversational Prayer

This form of prayer allows for the group members to pray in their own words in a way that is not intimidating. The group leader begins with Step One, inviting all to focus on the presence of Christ among them. After a few moments of quiet, the group leader invites anyone in the group to voice a prayer or two of thanksgiving; once that is complete, then anyone who has personal intentions may pray in their own words for their needs; finally, the group prays for the needs of others.

A suggested process:
In your own words, speak simple and short prayers to allow time for others to add their voices.

Focus on one "step" at a time, not worrying about praying for everything in your mental list at once.

Step One	Visualize Christ. Welcome him.
	Imagine him present with you in your group.
	Allow time for some silence.
Step Two	Gratitude opens our hearts.
	Use simple words such as, "Thank you, Lord, for . . ."
Step Three	Pray for your own needs knowing that others will pray with you.
	Be specific and honest.
	Use "I" and "me" language.

Step Four	Pray for others by name, with love.
	You may voice your agreement ("Yes, Lord").
	End with gratitude for sharing concerns.

Praying Like Ignatius

St. Ignatius Loyola, whose life and ministry are the foundation of the Jesuit community, invites us to enter into Scripture texts in order to experience the scenes, especially scenes of the gospels or other narrative parts of Scripture. Simply put, this is a method of creatively imagining the scene, viewing it from the inside, and asking God to meet you there. Most often, this is a personal form of prayer, but in a group setting, some of its elements can be helpful if you allow time for this process.

A suggested process:

- Select a scene from the chapters in the particular lesson.
- Read that scene out loud in the group, followed by some quiet time.
- Ask group members to place themselves in the scene (as a character, or as an onlooker) so that they can imagine the emotions, responses, and thinking that may have taken place. Notice the details and the tone, and imagine the interaction with the Lord that is taking place.
- Share with the group any insights that came to you in this quiet imagining.
- Allow each person in the group to thank God for some insight and to pray about some request that may have surfaced.

Sacred Reading (or Lectio Divina)

This method of prayer invites us to "listen with the ear of the heart" as St. Benedict's rule would say. We listen to the words and the phrasing, asking God to speak to our innermost being. Again, this method of prayer is most often used in an individual setting but may also be used in an adapted way within a group.

A suggested process:

- Select a scene from the chapters in the particular lesson.
- Read the scene out loud in the group, perhaps two times.
- Ask group members to ponder a word or phrase that stands out to them.
- The group members could then simply speak the word or phrase as a kind of litany of what was meaningful for your group.
- Allow time for more silence to ponder the words that were heard, asking God to reveal to you what message you are meant to hear, how God is speaking to you.
- Follow up with spoken intentions at the close of this group time.

REFLECTING ON SCRIPTURE

Reading Scripture is an opportunity not simply to learn new information but to listen to God who loves you. Pray that the same Holy Spirit who guided the formation of Scripture will inspire you to correctly understand what you read, and empower you to make what you read a part of your life.

The inspired word of God contains layers of meaning. As you make your way through passages of Scripture, whether studying a book of the Bible or focusing on a biblical theme, you may find it helpful to ask yourself these four questions:

What does the Scripture passage say?
Read the passage slowly and reflectively. Become familiar with it. If the passage you are reading is a narrative, carefully observe the characters and the plot. Use your imagination to picture the scene or enter into it.

What does the Scripture passage mean?
Read the footnotes in your Bible and the commentary provided to help you understand what the sacred writers intended and what God wants to communicate by means of their words.

What does the Scripture passage mean to me?
Meditate on the passage. God's word is living and powerful. What is God saying to you? How does the Scripture passage apply to your life today?

What am I going to do about it?
Try to discover how God may be challenging you in this passage. An encounter with God contains a challenge to know God's will and follow it more closely in daily life. Ask the Holy Spirit to inspire not only your mind but your life with this living word.